GOD
AND STEPHEN
HAWKING

A Lion Book
an imprint of
Lion Hudson plc
Wilkinson House, Jordan Hill Road,
Oxford OX2 8DR, England
www.lionhudson.com
ISBN 978 0 7459 5549 0

First edition 2010
10 9 8 7 6 5 4 3 2 1 0

Acknowledgments

Scripture quotations taken from the Holy Bible, New
International Version, copyright © 1973, 1978, 1984
International Bible Society. Used by permission of
Zondervan and Hodder & Stoughton Limited. All
rights reserved. The 'NIV' and 'New International
Version' trademarks are registered in the United
States Patent and Trademark Office by International
Bible Society. Use of either trademark requires the
permission of International Bible Society.
UK trademark number 1448790.

A catalogue record for this book is available
from the British Library

Typeset in 9.5/12 Palatino
Printed and bound in the UK by CPI Cox & Wyman, Reading

GOD
AND STEPHEN HAWKING

WHOSE DESIGN IS IT ANYWAY?

JOHN C. LENNOX

*For Rachel, Jonathan and Benjamin,
gifts of the Creator, who have made of
me a father.*

Acknowledgments

My thanks are due to Professors Nigel Cutland
and Alister McGrath for constructive advice.

Contents

Preface

I have written this short book in the hope that it will assist my readers to understand some of the most important issues that lie at the heart of the contemporary debate about God and science. For that reason, I have tried to avoid technicality where possible, and concentrate on the logic of the argument. I believe that those of us who have been educated in mathematics and the natural sciences have a responsibility for the public understanding of science. In particular, we have a duty to point out that not all statements by scientists are statements of science, and so do not carry the authority of authentic science even though such authority is often erroneously ascribed to them.

Of course that applies to me, as much as to anyone else, so I would ask the reader to scrutinize the arguments I have used very carefully. I am a mathematician and this book is not about mathematics, so the correctness of any of the mathematical results I may have proved elsewhere is no guarantee of the correctness of what I have said here. I do, however, have confidence in my readers' ability to follow an argument to its conclusion. I therefore submit what I have written to their judgment.

Introduction

God is very much on the agenda these days. Scientists have made sure of it by publishing book after book, with titles like Francis Collins' *The Language of God*, Richard Dawkins' *The God Delusion*, Victor Stenger's *God: The Failed Hypothesis*, Robert Winston's *The Story of God*, and so on, and on.

Some of these books have been runaway best-sellers. People obviously want to hear what the scientists have to say. That is not surprising, for science has immense cultural and intellectual authority in our sophisticated modern world. This is, in part, because of its phenomenal success in generating technologies from which all of us benefit, and in part because of its capacity to inspire, by giving us increased insight into the wonders of the universe as communicated by beautifully made television documentaries.

For that reason many people, increasingly aware that the material spin-offs from science do not satisfy the deepest needs of their humanity, are turning to the scientists to see if they have anything to say about the big questions of existence: Why are we here? What is the purpose of life? Where are we going? Is this universe all that exists, or is there more?

And these questions inevitably make us think about God. So millions of us want to know what science has to say about God. Some of the above best-sellers are written by atheists. But, and this is the important thing, not all the authors are atheists. This tells us at once that it would be very naïve to write off the debate as the inevitable clash between science and religion. That "conflict" view of the matter has long since been discredited. Take, for example, the first author on our list, Francis Collins, the Director of the National Institute of Health in the USA, and former Head of the Human Genome Project. His predecessor as head of that project was Jim Watson, winner (with Francis Crick) of the Nobel Prize for discovering the double-helix structure of DNA. Collins is a Christian, Watson an atheist. They are both top-level scientists, which shows us that what divides them is not their science but their world-view. There is a real conflict, but it is not science versus religion. It is theism versus atheism, and there are scientists on both sides.

And that is what makes the debate all the more interesting, because we can then focus on the real question at stake: does science point towards God, away from God, or is it neutral on the issue?

One thing is clear straightaway. This remarkable surge of interest in God defies the so-called secularization hypothesis, which rashly assumed, in the wake of the Enlightenment, that religion would eventually decline and die out – in Europe at least. Indeed, it could well be that it is precisely the perceived failure of secularization that is driving the God question ever higher on the agenda.

According to distinguished journalists John Micklethwait and Adrian Wooldridge of *The Economist*, "God is Back"[1] – and not only for the uneducated. "In much of the world it is exactly the sort of upwardly-mobile, educated middle classes that Marx and Weber presumed would shed such superstitions who are driving

---

[1] *God is Back: How the Global Rise of Faith is Changing the World*, London, Allen Lane, 2009.

the explosion of faith."[2] This particular development has understandably proved infuriating for the secularists, especially the atheist scientists among them.

The protest is loudest in Europe, perhaps because atheists feel Europe is where they have most to lose. They are probably right; and there are signs that they are losing it. Richard Dawkins, still the pack leader, has been frantically turning up the volume from loud to shrill, as the logic of his argument fractures – at least so it would seem, even to many of his fellow atheists. He is determined to "raise the consciousness" of the public, by recruiting as many disciples as possible to spread his faith that atheism is the only intellectually respectable viewpoint on the market. His campaign has even extended to posters on bendy-buses[3] and atheist summer camps for children; not forgetting, of course, large lapel badges marked with a red "A" for "atheist", and any number of intelligently designed T-shirts.

Whether this campaign had anything to do with it or not I don't know, but one very powerful scientific voice has been added to the atheist choir – that of physicist Stephen Hawking. Around the world the headlines were full of it: "Stephen Hawking says universe not created by God", "Stephen Hawking says physics leaves no room for God", and so on with many variations. The headlines were referring to the publication of a new book by Hawking and his co-author Leonard Mlodinow, *The Grand Design*. It raced immediately to the top of the best-seller charts. The public confession of atheism by a

---

2 Op. cit. p. 18.
3 Sporting the message: "There's probably no God, now stop worrying and enjoy your life." Associating God with worry was surely a masterpiece of misrepresentation. I wonder who thought of it? And as for "probably"…

man of such high intellectual profile as Hawking has had the instant effect of ratcheting up the debate by several notches. It has also sold a lot of books.

What are we to think? Is that it, then? Is there nothing more to discuss? Should all theologians resign their chairs forthwith? Should all church workers hang up their hats and go home? Has the Grand Master of Physics checkmated the Grand Designer of the Universe?

It certainly is a grandiose claim to have banished God. After all, the majority of great scientists in the past have believed in him. Many still do. Were Galileo, Kepler, Newton and Maxwell, to name a few, really all wrong on the God question?

With such a lot at stake we surely need to ask Hawking to produce evidence to establish his claim. Do his arguments really stand up to close scrutiny? I think we have a right to know.

But we shall never know unless we look and see.

So, let us do just that...

1 The big questions

Stephen Hawking is, without doubt, the world's most famous living scientist. He has recently retired from the Lucasian Professorship in Cambridge, a chair once held by Sir Isaac Newton. Hawking has occupied this position with great distinction. He has been made a Companion of Honour by Her Majesty the Queen, and his academic career has been marked by an accolade of honorary degrees from all over the world.

He has also been an outstanding symbol of fortitude, having suffered the ravages of motor neurone disease for over forty years. During many of these he has been confined to a wheelchair, with his only means of verbal communication being a specially designed electronic voice synthesizer. Its instantly recognizable "voice" is known all over the world.

With many distinguished colleagues and students, Hawking has explored the frontiers of mathematical physics – most famously, perhaps, the counter-intuitive mysteries of black holes. His work has led to the prediction of "Hawking Radiation", which, if verified experimentally, would surely qualify him for a Nobel Prize.

In his runaway best-seller, *A Brief History of Time*[4], Hawking brought the recondite world of fundamental physics to the coffee table (although many people have confessed to finding the contents rather beyond them).

4   London, Bantam Press, 1988.

This book was followed by several others in the same vein, which attempted quite successfully to excite a wider readership with the buzz of great science.

Since his books deal with the origin of the universe, it was inevitable that he should consider the matter of the existence of a Divine Creator. However, *A Brief History of Time* left this matter tantalizingly open, by ending with the much-quoted statement that if physicists were to find a "Theory of Everything" (that is, a theory that unified the four fundamental forces of nature: the strong and weak nuclear forces, electromagnetism and gravity), we would "know the Mind of God".

In his latest book, *The Grand Design*[5], co-authored with Leonard Mlodinow[6], Hawking's reticence has disappeared, and he challenges belief in the divine creation of the universe. According to him it is the laws of physics, not the will of God, that provide the real explanation as to how the universe came into being. The Big Bang, he argues, was the inevitable consequence of these laws: "because there is a law such as gravity, the universe can and will create itself from nothing".

The title, *The Grand Design*, will suggest for many people the existence of a Grand Designer – but that is actually what the book is designed to deny. Hawking's grand conclusion is: "Spontaneous creation is the reason there is something rather than nothing, why the universe exists, why we exist. It is not necessary to invoke God to light the blue touch paper and set the universe going."[7]

---

[5] London, Bantam Press, 2010.

[6] From here on I shall refer to Hawking's book. I adopt this convention simply for convenience of expression. No disrespect is intended for the co-author, Leonard Mlodinow.

[7] Op. cit. p. 180.

In this book I wish to engage in the main not with Hawking's science but with what he deduces from it regarding the existence, or rather the non-existence, of God. Although Hawking's argument, that science shows God is unnecessary, has been hailed as ground-breaking, it is hardly new. For years other scientists have made similar claims, maintaining that the awesome, sophisticated complexity of the world around us can be interpreted solely by reference to the basic stuff of the universe (mass/energy), or to the physical laws that describe the behaviour of the universe, such as the law of gravity. Indeed, it is difficult at first glance to see quite how this new book adds much to what Hawking wrote in *A Brief History of Time*.

The Grand Design opens with a list of the big questions that people have always asked: "How can we understand the world in which we find ourselves? How does the universe behave? What is the nature of reality? Where did all this come from? Did the universe need a Creator?"[8] These questions, emanating from such a famous person, excite the imagination with the anticipation of hearing a world-class scientist give his insights on some of the profoundest questions of metaphysics. It is, after all, fascinating to listen in on a great mind exploring the philosophical questions that we all ask from time to time.

An inadequate view of philosophy

If that is what we expect we are in for a shock; for, in his very next words, Hawking dismisses philosophy.

---

8   Op. cit. p. 5.

Referring to his list of questions, he writes: "Traditionally these are questions for philosophy, but philosophy is dead. It has not kept up with modern developments in science, particularly in physics. As a result scientists have become the bearers of the torch of discovery in our quest for knowledge."[9]

Apart from the unwarranted hubris of this dismissal of philosophy (a discipline well represented and respected at his own university of Cambridge), it constitutes rather disturbing evidence that at least one scientist, Hawking himself, has not even kept up with philosophy sufficiently to realize that he himself is engaging in it throughout his book.

For, the very first thing I notice is that Hawking's statement about philosophy is itself a philosophical statement. It is manifestly not a statement of science: it is a metaphysical statement *about* science. Therefore, his statement that philosophy is dead contradicts itself. It is a classic example of logical incoherence.

Furthermore, the view that "scientists have become the bearers of the torch of discovery" smacks of scientism – the view that science is the only way to truth. It is a conviction characteristic of that movement in secular thought known as the "New Atheism", although its ideas are mostly only new in the aggressive way they are presented, rather than in their intellectual content.

For any scientist, let alone a science superstar, to disparage philosophy on the one hand, and then at once to adopt a self-contradictory philosophical stance on the other, is not the wisest thing to do – especially at the beginning of a book that is designed to be convincing.

9   Op. cit. p. 5.

Nobel Laureate Sir Peter Medawar pointed out this danger long ago in his excellent book *Advice to a Young Scientist*, which ought to be compulsory reading for all scientists.

> There is no quicker way for a scientist to bring discredit upon himself and upon his profession than roundly to declare – particularly when no declaration of any kind is called for – that science knows, or soon will know, the answers to all questions worth asking, and that questions which do not admit a scientific answer are in some way non-questions or "pseudo-questions" that only simpletons ask and only the gullible profess to be able to answer.

Medawar goes on to say: "The existence of a limit to science is, however, made clear by its inability to answer childlike elementary questions having to do with first and last things – questions such as: 'How did everything begin?' 'What are we all here for?' 'What is the point of living?'"[10] He adds that we must turn to imaginative literature and religion for the answers to such questions.

Francis Collins is equally clear on the limitations of science: "Science is powerless to answer questions such as 'Why did the universe come into being?' 'What is the meaning of human existence?' 'What happens after we die?' "[11]

Obviously Medawar and Collins are passionate scientists. So there is clearly no inconsistency involved

---

[10] *Advice to a Young Scientist*, London, Harper and Row, 1979, p. 31; see also his book *The Limits of Science*, Oxford, Oxford University Press, 1984, p. 66.
[11] *The Language of God*, New York, The Free Press, 2006.

in being a committed scientist at the highest level, while simultaneously recognizing that science cannot answer every kind of question, including some of the deepest questions that human beings can ask.

For instance, there is widespread acknowledgment that it is very difficult to get a base for morality in science. Albert Einstein saw this clearly. In a discussion on science and religion in Berlin in 1930, he said that our human sense of beauty and our religious instinct are "tributary forms in helping the reasoning faculty towards its highest achievements. You are right in speaking of the moral foundations of science, but you cannot turn round and speak of the scientific foundations of morality." Einstein proceeded to point out that science cannot form a base for morality: "every attempt to reduce ethics to scientific formulae must fail".[12]

Richard Feynman, also a Nobel Prize-winning physicist, shared Einstein's view: "Even the greatest forces and abilities don't seem to carry any clear instructions on how to use them. As an example, the great accumulation of understanding as to how the physical world behaves only convinces one that this behaviour has a kind of meaninglessness about it. The sciences do not directly teach good or bad."[13] Elsewhere he states that "ethical values lie outside the scientific realm".[14]

Yet Hawking seems to deny this, by assigning to science a role beyond its capacity. Not only that but, after disparaging philosophy, he then proceeds to engage in it. For, insofar as he is interpreting and applying science

---

[12] For this and Einstein's stance on religion and science see the definitive work of Max Jammer, *Einstein and Religion*, Princeton, Princeton University Press, 1999. The citation here is from p. 69.

[13] *The Meaning of It All*, London, Penguin, 2007, p. 32.

[14] Op. cit. p. 43.

to ultimate questions like the existence of God, Hawking is doing metaphysics. Now, let us be clear, I do not fault him for doing that; I shall be engaging in metaphysics all through this book. My concern is that he does not seem to recognize this.

Let's look a little more closely at Hawking's two lists of questions. Here is the first list:

- How can we understand the world in which we find ourselves?
- How does the universe behave?
- What is the nature of reality?
- Where did all this come from?
- Did the universe need a Creator?[15]

The second of these questions is scientific: a typical "how" question that does not raise the matter of ultimate purpose. The first and the last three questions are fundamental questions of philosophy.

Hawking's second list is to be found at the end of his first chapter:

- Why is there something rather than nothing?
- Why do we exist?
- Why this particular set of laws and not some other?[16]

These are also well-known great questions of philosophy.

Now science, of course, is one of the voices that will have an input into attempting to answer these questions; but it is by no means the only, nor indeed necessarily the most important, voice.

---

15 Op. cit. p. 5.
16 Op. cit. p. 10.

Philosophy may be dead according to Hawking, but he seems to believe in giving it an immediate resurrection! Calling his three questions "The Ultimate Questions of Life, the Universe and Everything", Hawking says: "We shall attempt to answer them in this book."

An inadequate view of God

The consequence of sailing through one red light is that you are likely to sail through a good many more, and that is exactly what happens. Hawking's inadequate view of philosophy soon shows itself in an inadequate view of God. He writes: "Ignorance of nature's ways led people in ancient times to invent gods to lord it over every aspect of human life." He then says that this began to change with ancient Greek thinkers like Thales of Miletus about 2,600 years ago: "The idea arose that nature follows consistent principles that could be deciphered. And so began the long process of replacing the notion of the reign of the gods with the concept of the notion of a universe that is governed by laws of nature, and created according to a blueprint we could someday learn to read."[17]

The impression given by this is that the concept of God, or the gods, is a placeholder for human ignorance – a "God of the Gaps", who will increasingly be displaced as the gaps in our knowledge are filled by scientific explanations, so that he will eventually disappear completely, like the smile on the face of the proverbial Cheshire cat. In the past there have been many gaps in

[17] Op. cit. p. 17.

the scientific picture that have been occupied by God; but Hawking now claims that physics has no longer any room for God, as it has removed the last place where he might be found – the moment of creation. The last piece of the scientific jigsaw has been snapped into place and it leaves us with a closed universe.

He is but a step away from regarding atheism as a necessary prerequisite for doing science.

First of all, let us look at the element of truth in what Hawking says. When it thunders, if we suppose that it is a god roaring – as some of the ancients did – we would scarcely be in a mood to investigate the mechanism behind the noise. Only by assuming that there are no gods of this kind can we be free to investigate the mechanisms of nature in a scientific manner.

So we certainly need to remove deification of the forces of nature in order to be free to study nature. This was a revolutionary step in thinking, taken, as Hawking points out, by early Greek natural philosophers like Thales, Anaximander, and Anaximenes of Milesia over 2,500 years ago.

They were not content with mythological explanations, such as those written down by Homer and Hesiod around 700 BC. They sought explanations in terms of natural processes and chalked up some notable scientific successes. Thales is accredited with calculating the length of the year as 365 days, accurately predicting a solar eclipse in 585 BC, and using geometric methods to calculate the height of pyramids from their shadows, and even to estimate the size of the earth and moon. Anaximander invented a sundial and a weatherproof clock, and made the first world and star maps. The Milesians were therefore among the earliest "scientists", although the word "scientist" was first introduced (by William Whewell) in the nineteenth century.

Of great interest in the present context is Xenophanes (c. 570–478 BC) of Colophon (near Izmir in present-day Turkey), who, though he was known for his attempts to understand the significance of the fossils of sea creatures found in Malta, is even more famous for his trenchant denunciation of the mythological world-view. He pointed out that certain behaviour was attributed to the gods which would be regarded as utterly shameful among humans: the gods were rogues, thieves, and adulterers. Not unreasonably, Xenophanes held that these gods had been made in the images of the peoples that believed in them: Ethiopians have gods that are dark and flat-nosed, Thracians made them blue-eyed and red-haired. He added derisively: "If cows and horses or lions had hands and could draw, then horses would draw the forms of gods like horses, cows like cows, making their bodies similar in shape to their own." Thus, for Xenophanes, these gods were but childish fiction drawn from the fertile imaginations of those who believed in them.

Furthermore, the influential Greek atomist philosopher, Epicurus (born in 341 BC just after the death of Plato), who gave his name to Epicurean philosophy, wished to remove the myths from explanation in order to improve understanding: "Thunderbolts can be produced in several different ways – just be sure the myths are kept out of it! And they will be kept out of it if one follows rightly the appearances and takes them as signs of what is unobservable."

Such denunciation of the gods, together with a determination to investigate the natural processes hitherto almost exclusively understood to be the activity of those gods, inevitably led to the decline of mythological interpretations of the universe and paved the way for scientific advance.

Xenophanes was, however, not the only ancient thinker to criticize the polytheistic world-view. More importantly, he wasn't the first to do so. Unknown to him presumably (there does not seem to be much information on the matter), and centuries beforehand, the Hebrew leader Moses had warned against worshipping "other gods, bowing down to them or to the sun or the moon or the stars of the sky". Later, the prophet Jeremiah, writing in about 600 BC, similarly denounced the absurdity of deifying nature and worshipping the sun, moon and stars.

We now reach a crucial error that seems to have escaped Hawking's attention. It is to imagine that getting rid of gods either necessitates, or is the same as, getting rid of God. Far from it. For Moses and the Hebrew prophets it was absurd to bow down to various bits of the universe, like the sun, moon and stars, as gods. But they regarded it equally as absurd not to believe in, and bow down to, the Creator God who had made both the universe and them.

Nor were they introducing a radically novel idea. They did not have to have their universe de-deified as the Greeks did, for the simple reason that they had never believed in such gods. What had saved them from that superstition was their belief in the One True God, Creator of heaven and earth. What Moses and the prophets were protesting about was the *introduction* of the gods into a previously monotheistic culture.

That is, the idolatrous and polytheistic universe described by Homer and Hesiod was not the original world-picture of humankind. Nevertheless, this is an impression often gained from books on science and philosophy (including *The Grand Design*) that start with the ancient Greeks and rightly emphasize the importance of the de-deification of the universe, yet singularly fail to point out that the Hebrews had vigorously protested against idolatrous interpretations of the universe long before the time of the Greeks. This obscures the fact that polytheism arguably constitutes a perversion of an original belief in the One Creator God. It was this perversion that needed to be corrected, by recovering belief in the Creator and not by jettisoning it. The same is true today.

In order to avoid confusion, we should explore the depth of the gulf between the Greek and Hebrew views of the universe a little further, just to see how vast and unbridgeable it is. Commenting on Hesiod's poem "Theogony" ("The genesis of the gods"), Werner Jaeger writes:

> If we compare this Greek hypostasis of the world-creative Eros with that of the Logos in the Hebrew account of creation, we may observe a deep-lying difference in the outlook of the two peoples. The Logos is a substantialization of an intellectual property or power of God the creator, who is stationed outside the world and brings that world into existence by his own personal fiat. The Greek gods are stationed inside the world; they are descended from Heaven and Earth ... they are generated by the mighty power of Eros who likewise belongs within the world as an all-engendering primitive force. Thus they are already subject to what we should call natural law

... When Hesiod's thought at last gives way to truly philosophical thinking, the Divine is sought inside the world – not outside it, as in the Jewish Christian theology that develops out of the book of Genesis.[18]

It is therefore a very striking fact that Xenophanes, despite being steeped in a polytheistic culture, did not make the mistake of confusing God with the gods and thus reject the former with the latter. He believed in one God who ruled the universe. He wrote: "There is one God ... similar to mortals neither in shape nor in thought ... remote and effortless he governs all there is."

Hawking is surely not expecting us to fall for the common trick of rubbishing religion by rubbishing primitive concepts of God or the gods. Yet, whether deliberately or not, he confuses God with the gods. And that inevitably leads him to a completely inadequate view of God, as a God of the Gaps who can be displaced by scientific advance. It is, however, a view of God that is not to be found in any major monotheistic religion, where God is not a God of the Gaps but the author of the whole show. Nor, incidentally, is he the God of the deists, who lit the blue touch paper to start the universe going and then retired to a vast uninvolved distance. God both created the universe and constantly sustains it in existence. Without him, nothing would be there for physicists like Stephen Hawking and Leonard Mlodinow to study.

In particular, therefore, God is the creator both of the bits of the universe we don't understand and of

---

[18] *The Theology of the Early Greek Philosophers*, Oxford, Oxford University Press, 1967 paperback, pp. 16–17.

the bits that we do. And it is, of course, the bits that we do understand that give the most evidence of God's existence and activity. Just as my admiration of the genius behind a work of engineering or art increases the more I understand it, so my worship of the Creator increases the more I understand the universe he has created.

2 God or the laws of nature?

A matter of logic: a self-creating universe?

One of the main conclusions of *The Grand Design* is: "Because there is a law of gravity, the universe can and will create itself out of nothing."[19] First, a general comment on this key expression of Hawking's belief.

According to him, as we have seen, philosophy is dead. However, one of the main tasks of philosophy is to train people in the art of definition, logical analysis, and argument. Is Hawking really telling us that this also is dead? Surely not. However, it would seem that some of his arguments could have profited from a little more attention to the matter of clarity of definition and logical analysis. We shall start with the statement just quoted.

The first question to ask is: what does Hawking mean when he uses the word "nothing" in the statement "the universe can and will create itself out of nothing"? Note the assumption in the first part of that statement: "Because there is a law of gravity…" Hawking assumes, therefore, that a law of gravity exists. One presumes also that he believes that gravity itself exists, for the simple

19 Op. cit. p. 180.

reason that an abstract mathematical law on its own would be vacuous with nothing to describe – a point to which we shall return. The main issue for now, however, is that gravity or a law of gravity is not "nothing", if he is using that word in its usual philosophically correct sense of "non-being". If he is not, he should have told us.

On the face of it, Hawking appears, therefore, to be simultaneously asserting that the universe is created from nothing and from something – not a very promising start. Indeed, one might add for good measure the fact that when physicists talk about "nothing", they often appear to mean a quantum vacuum, which is manifestly not nothing. In fact, Hawking is surely alluding to this when he writes: "We are a product of quantum fluctuations in the very early universe."[20]

Later on in the book he sets the total energy of empty space to zero by subtracting the actual value and then seems to proceed on the assumption that the energy actually is zero when he asks the question: "If the total energy of the universe must always remain zero, and it costs energy to create a body, how can a whole universe be created from nothing?"[21] This seems, at least to me, a rather dubious move.

Could all of this be just a little too "much ado about nothing"?

The situation does not improve when we move on to the logic of the second part of Hawking's statement: "the universe can and will create itself from nothing". This assertion is self-contradictory. If we say "X creates Y", we presuppose the existence of X in the first place in order to bring Y into existence. That is a simple matter

[20] Op. cit. p. 139.

[21] Op. cit. p. 180.

of understanding what the words "X creates Y" mean. If, therefore, we say "X creates X", we imply that we are presupposing the existence of X in order to account for the existence of X. This is obviously self-contradictory and thus logically incoherent – even if we put X equal to the universe! To presuppose the existence of the universe to account for its own existence sounds like something out of *Alice in Wonderland*, not science.

It is seldom that one finds in a single statement two distinct levels of contradiction, but Hawking appears to have constructed such a statement. He says the universe comes from a nothing that turns out to be a something (self-contradiction number one), and then he says the universe creates itself (self-contradiction number two). But that is not all. His notion that a law of nature (gravity) explains the existence of the universe is also self-contradictory, since a law of nature, by definition, surely depends for its own existence on the prior existence of the nature it purports to describe. More on what laws are later.

Thus, the main conclusion of the book turns out not simply to be a self-contradiction, which would be disaster enough, but to be a triple self-contradiction. Philosophers just might be tempted to comment: so that is what comes of saying philosophy is dead!

In the above, Hawking is echoing the language of Oxford chemist Peter Atkins (also a well-known atheist), who believes that "space-time generates its own dust in the process of its own self-assembly".[22] Atkins dubs this the "Cosmic Bootstrap" principle, referring to the self-contradictory idea of a person lifting himself by pulling on his own bootlaces. His Oxford colleague, philosopher

---

[22]   *Creation Revisited*, Harmondsworth, Penguin, 1994, p. 143.

of religion Keith Ward, is surely right to say that Atkins' view of the universe is as blatantly self-contradictory as the name he gives to it, pointing out that it is "logically impossible for a cause to bring about some effect without already being in existence". Ward concludes: "Between the hypothesis of God and the hypothesis of a cosmic bootstrap, there is no competition. We were always right to think that persons, or universes, who seek to pull themselves up by their own bootstraps are forever doomed to failure."[23]

What this all goes to show is that nonsense remains nonsense, even when talked by world-famous scientists. What serves to obscure the illogicality of such statements is the fact that they are made by scientists; and the general public, not surprisingly, assumes that they are statements of science and takes them on authority. That is why it is important to point out that they are not statements of science, and any statement, whether made by a scientist or not, should be open to logical analysis. Immense prestige and authority does not compensate for faulty logic.

The worrying thing is that this illogical notion of the universe creating itself is not some peripheral point in *The Grand Design*. It appears to be a key argument. And if the key argument is invalid, in one sense there is little left to say.

However, since the laws of nature (gravity in particular) play a major role in Hawking's argument, it will be important to comment on what look very much like serious misunderstandings regarding the nature and capacity of such laws.

[23] *God, Chance and Necessity*, Oxford, One World Publications, 1996, p. 49.

The nature of the laws of nature

Hawking points out that there was originally no clear distinction in Greek thought between human laws and the laws of nature; and he gives the classic example of Heraclitus (c.535–c.475 BC), who thought that the sun's movement in the sky was occasioned by its fear of being hunted down by a vengeful goddess of justice. The idea that inanimate objects possessed minds and intentionality was espoused by Aristotle, and dominated Western thinking for around 2,000 years.

Hawking reminds us that it was Descartes (1596–1650) who first formulated the concept of the laws of nature in our contemporary sense. Here is Hawking's definition of a law of nature: "Today most scientists would say that a law of nature is a rule that is based upon an observed regularity and provides predictions that go beyond the immediate situations upon which it is based."[24] A familiar example of such a law is "the sun rises in the east". It is based on an observed regularity, and predicts that the sun will rise in the east tomorrow. On the other hand, "swans are white" is not a law of nature. Not all swans are white; the next one we see may well be black.

Of course, saying that "the sun rises in the east" is a law rests on a number of unspoken assumptions. As David Hume, the Scottish Enlightenment philosopher, pointed out, the fact that we have observed the sun to rise a thousand times in the past does not prove that it will rise again tomorrow. We have to add something like, "all things being equal", "provided the sun does not explode", etc.

[24]   Op. cit. p. 27.

In fact, the apparently simple concept of a law of nature turns out to be anything but simple. Must laws be universally exact and exceptionless to qualify as laws? Think of Newton's famous laws of motion. They are accurate enough to facilitate the calculations needed to effect a moon landing; but they cannot cope with velocities near that of light, where Einstein's more accurate relativity theory is needed.

In other words, it is not enough to state Newton's laws on their own. We need additionally to specify at least the range of conditions under which they are valid.

The origin of the laws of nature

Hawking has three questions to ask about the laws of nature:[25]
- What is the origin of these laws?
- Are there any exceptions to the laws, i.e. miracles?
- Is there only one set of possible laws?

Hawking suggests that the traditional answer to the first question, given by the great pioneers of science like Galileo, Kepler, Descartes and Newton, is that the laws are the work of God. Hawking adds: "However, this is no more than a definition of God as the embodiment of the laws of nature. Unless one endows God with some other attributes, such as being the God of the Old Testament, employing God as a response to the first question merely substitutes one mystery for another."[26]

[25] Op. cit. p. 29.
[26] Op. cit. p. 29.

However, the God in whom Galileo, Kepler, Descartes and Newton believed was not merely the embodiment of the laws of nature. He was (and is) the intelligent Creator and upholder of the universe, who is a person and not a set of abstract laws. He was, in fact, the God of the Bible. Hawking's statement, therefore, seems somewhat confused.

I spoke earlier of Newton's laws, and not God's laws. The reason for doing that is simple. It was Newton who formulated the laws that encapsulated the behaviour of bodies in motion under certain conditions. Newton's laws describe the regularities, the pattern, to which motion in the universe conforms under certain initial conditions. It was God, however, and not Newton who created the universe with those regularities and patterns. It was also God who ultimately was responsible for the intellectual power and insight of the mind of Newton that recognized the patterns and gave them elegant mathematical formulation. The laws were therefore, in that sense, the work of Newton.

It would surely sound rather foolish to say that, in ascribing the laws to Newton, it is no more than a definition of Newton as the embodiment of the laws of nature. It does not sound any less foolish when applied to God. Some people may wish to define God as the laws of nature. Indeed it seems to me that Hawking is effectively doing just that when he assigns creatorial powers to those laws. That inadequate view of God is surely not what Galileo, Kepler, Newton and Descartes believed.

God or the laws of physics?

Hawking's faulty concept of God as a "God of the Gaps" now has serious consequences. This "more science, therefore less God" kind of thinking inevitably leads Hawking to make the mistake (frequently made by Richard Dawkins and others) of asking us to choose between God and science; or, in Hawking's specific case, between God and the laws of physics. Talking about M-theory (his chosen candidate for a final unifying theory of physics), Hawking writes: "M-theory predicts that a great many universes were created out of nothing. Their creation does not require the intervention of some supernatural being or god. Rather, these multiple universes arise naturally from physical law."[27]

A supernatural being or god is an agent who does something. In the case of the God of the Bible, he is a personal agent. Dismissing such an agent, Hawking ascribes creative power to physical law; but physical law is not an agent. Hawking is making a classic category mistake by confusing two entirely different kinds of entity: physical law and personal agency. The choice he sets before us is between false alternatives. He has confused two levels of explanation: agency and law. God is an explanation of the universe, but not the same type of explanation as that which is given by physics.

Suppose, to make matters clearer, we replace the universe by a jet engine and then are asked to explain it. Shall we account for it by mentioning the personal agency of its inventor, Sir Frank Whittle? Or shall we follow Hawking: dismiss personal agency, and explain

27   Op. cit. pp. 8–9.

the jet engine by saying that it arose naturally from physical law?

It is clearly nonsensical to ask people to choose *between* Frank Whittle and science as an explanation for the jet engine. For it is not a question of either/or. It is self-evident that we need *both* levels of explanation in order to give a complete description. It is also obvious that the scientific explanation neither conflicts nor competes with the agent explanation: they complement one another. It is the same with explanations of the universe: God does not conflict or compete with the laws of physics as an explanation. God is actually the ground of all explanation, in the sense that he is the cause in the first place of there being a world for the laws of physics to describe.

Offering people the choice between God and science is therefore illogical. In addition, it is very unwise, because some people might just choose God and then Hawking could be accused of putting people off science!

Sir Isaac Newton, a previous holder of the Lucasian Chair at Cambridge, did not make Hawking's category mistake when he discovered his law of gravitation. Newton did not say: "Now that I have the law of gravity, I don't need God." What he did was to write *Principia Mathematica*, the most famous book in the history of science, expressing the hope that it would "persuade the thinking man" to believe in God.

The laws of physics can explain how the jet engine works, but not how it came to exist in the first place. It is self-evident that the laws of physics could not have created a jet engine on their own. That task also needed the intelligence, imagination, and scientific creativity of Whittle. Indeed, even the laws of physics plus Frank

Whittle were not sufficient to produce a jet engine. There also needed to be some material that Whittle could use. Matter may be humble stuff, but laws cannot create it.

Millennia ago Aristotle thought a great deal about these issues. He spoke about four different "causes" that we can, perhaps, reasonably translate informally as "levels of explanation". Thinking of the jet engine, first there is the material cause – the raw material out of which the engine is crafted; then there is the formal cause – the concept, plan, theory, and blueprint that Sir Frank Whittle conceived and to which he worked. Next there is the efficient cause – Sir Frank Whittle himself, who did the work. Fourthly, and last in the list, there is the final cause – the ultimate purpose for which the jet engine was conceived and built: to power a particular aircraft to fly faster than ever before.

The example of the jet engine can help us to clear up another confusion. Science, according to many scientists, concentrates essentially on material causation. It asks the "how" questions: how does the jet engine work? It also asks the "why" question regarding function: why is this pipe here? But it does not ask the "why" question of purpose: why was the jet engine built? What is important here is that Sir Frank Whittle does not appear in the scientific account. To quote Laplace, the scientific account has "no need of that hypothesis".[28] Clearly, however, it would be ridiculous to deduce from this that Whittle did not exist. He is the answer to the question: why does the jet engine exist in the first place?

---

[28] However, the answer to some of these questions *may constitute scientific evidence for* the input of an external intelligence – a matter that I pursue in some detail in *God's Undertaker*, see e.g. p. 11.

Yet this is essentially what many scientists (and others) do with God. They define the range of questions that science is permitted to ask in such a way that God is excluded from the start; and then they claim that God is unnecessary, or doesn't exist. They fail to see that their science does not answer the question as to why something exists rather than nothing, for the simple reason that their science cannot answer that question. They also fail to see that by assumption it is their atheist world-view, not science as such, that excludes God.

The scientists did not put the universe there. But neither did their theories, nor the laws of mathematical physics. Yet Hawking seems to think they did. In *A Brief History of Time* he hinted at this kind of explanation, suggesting that a theory might bring the universe into existence:

> The usual approach of science of constructing a mathematical model cannot answer the questions of why there should be a universe for the model to describe. Why does the universe go to all the bother of existing? Is the unified theory so compelling that it brings about its own existence? Or does it need a creator, and, if so, does he have any other effect on the universe?[29]

Much as I find it hard to believe, Hawking seems to wish to reduce all explanation to formal causes only. He claims that all that is necessary to create the universe is the law of gravity. When asked[30] where gravity came from, he answered: "M-theory." However, to say that a theory or physical laws could bring the universe (or anything at

---

[29] Op. cit. p. 174.
[30] *Larry King Live*, 10 September 2010.

all, for that matter) into existence is to misunderstand what theory and laws are. Scientists expect to develop theories involving mathematical laws to describe natural phenomena, which enable them to make predictions; and they have done so with spectacular success. However, on their own, the theories and laws cannot even *cause* anything, let alone *create* it.

Long ago none other than the Christian philosopher William Paley said as much. Speaking of the person who had just stumbled on a watch on the heath and picked it up, he says that such a person would not be

> less surprised to be informed that the watch in his hand was nothing more than the result of the laws of *metallic* nature. It is a perversion of language to assign any law as the efficient, operative cause of any thing. A law presupposes an agent; for it is only the mode, according to which an agent proceeds: it implies a power; for it is the order, according to which that power acts. Without this agent, without this power, which are both distinct from itself, the *law* does nothing; is nothing.[31]

Quite so. Physical laws cannot create anything. They are a description of what normally happens under certain given conditions. This is surely obvious from the very first example that Hawking gives of physical law. The sun rises in the east every day, but this law does not create the sun; nor the planet earth, with east and west. The law is descriptive and predictive, but it is not creative. Similarly Newton's law of gravitation does not

---

[31] William Paley, *Natural Theology*, 1802, p. 7.

create gravity or the matter on which gravity acts. In fact, Newton's law does not even *explain* gravity, as Newton himself realized.

The laws of physics are not only incapable of creating anything; they cannot even *cause* anything to happen. For instance, Newton's celebrated laws of motion never caused a pool ball to race across the green baize table. That can only be done by people using a pool cue and the actions of their own muscles. The laws enable us to analyse the motion, and to map the trajectory of the ball's movement in the future (provided nothing external interferes); but they are powerless to move the ball, let alone bring it into existence.

One can understand what is meant by saying that the behaviour of the universe is governed by the laws of nature. But what can Hawking possibly mean by saying that the universe arises naturally from physical law, or that gravity arises from M-theory?

Another example of this basic misunderstanding of the nature of law is given by well-known physicist Paul Davies: "There's no need to invoke anything supernatural in the origins of the universe or of life. I have never liked the idea of divine tinkering: for me it is much more inspiring to believe that a set of mathematical laws can be so clever as to bring all these things into being."[32]

However, in the world in which most of us live, the simple law of arithmetic by itself, 1+1=2, never brought anything into being. It certainly has never put any money into my bank account. If I put £1,000 into the bank, and later another £1,000, the laws of arithmetic will rationally explain how it is that I now have £2,000 in the bank. But if

---

[32] Cited by Clive Cookson, "Scientists who glimpsed God", *Financial Times*, 29 April 1995, p. 20.

I never put any money into the bank myself, and simply leave it to the laws of arithmetic to bring money into being in my bank account, I shall remain permanently bankrupt.

C. S. Lewis grasped this issue, with characteristic clarity. Of the laws of nature he writes:

> They produce no events: they state the pattern to which every event – if only it can be induced to happen – must conform, just as the rules of arithmetic state the pattern to which all transactions with money must conform – if only you can get hold of any money. Thus in one sense the laws of Nature cover the whole field of space and time; in another, what they leave out is precisely the whole real universe – the incessant torrent of actual events which makes up true history. That must come from somewhere else. To think the laws can produce it is like thinking that you can create real money by simply doing sums. For every law, in the last resort, says: "If you have A, then you will get B." But first catch your A: the laws won't do it for you.
>
> Laws give us only a universe of "Ifs and Ands": not this universe which actually exists. What we know through laws and general principles is a series of connections. But, in order for there to be a real universe, the connections must be given something to connect; a torrent of opaque actualities must be fed into the pattern. If God created the world then He is precisely the source of this torrent, and it alone gives our truest principles anything to be true *about*. But if God is the ultimate source of all concrete, individual things and events, then God Himself must be

concrete, and individual in the highest degree.
Unless the origin of all other things were itself
concrete and individual, nothing else could be
so; for there is no conceivable means whereby
what is abstract or general could itself produce
concrete reality. Book-keeping, continued to all
eternity, could never produce one farthing.[33]

The world of strict naturalism, in which clever
mathematical laws all by themselves bring the universe
and life into existence, is pure (science) fiction. Theories
and laws do not bring matter/energy into existence. The
view that nevertheless they somehow have that capacity
seems a rather desperate refuge from the alternative
possibility implied by Hawking's question cited above:
"Or does it need a Creator?"

If Hawking were not as dismissive of philosophy
he might have come across the Wittgenstein statement
that the "deception of modernism" is the idea that the
laws of nature *explain* the world to us, when all they do
is *describe* structural regularities. Richard Feynman, a
Nobel Laureate in physics, takes the matter further:

The fact that there are rules at all to be checked is
a kind of miracle; that it is possible to find a rule,
like the inverse square law of gravitation, is some
sort of miracle. It is not understood at all, but it
leads to the possibility of prediction – that means
it tells you what you would expect to happen in an
experiment you have not yet done.[34]

---

33 *Miracles*, London, Fontana, 1974, pp. 63, 90–91.
34 *The Meaning of It All*, London, Penguin, 2007, p. 23.

The very fact that those laws can be mathematically formulated was for Einstein a constant source of amazement that pointed beyond the physical universe. He wrote: "Every one who is seriously engaged in the pursuit of science becomes convinced that the laws of nature manifest the existence of a spirit vastly superior to that of men, and one in the face of which we with our modest powers must feel humble."[35]

Hawking has signally failed to answer the central question: why is there something rather than nothing? He says that the existence of gravity means the creation of the universe was inevitable. But how did gravity come to exist in the first place? What was the creative force behind its birth? Who put it there, with all its properties and potential for mathematical description in terms of law? Similarly, when Hawking argues in support of his theory of spontaneous creation, that it was only necessary for "the blue touch paper" to be lit to "set the universe going", I am tempted to ask: where did this blue touch paper come from? It is clearly not part of the universe, if it set the universe going. So who lit it, in the sense of ultimate causation, if not God?

Allan Sandage, widely regarded as the father of modern astronomy, discoverer of quasars, and winner of the Crafoord Prize (astronomy's equivalent of the Nobel Prize), is in no doubt about his answer: "I find it quite improbable that such order came out of chaos. There has to be some organizing principle. God to me is a mystery but is the explanation for the miracle of existence – why there is something rather than nothing."[36]

---

[35] Letter of 24 January 1936 to a schoolgirl, Phyllis Wright.

[36] *New York Times*, 12 March 1991, p. B9.

It is fascinating that Hawking, in attacking religion, feels compelled to put so much emphasis on the Big Bang theory, because, even if the non-believers don't like it, the Big Bang resonates powerfully with the biblical narrative of creation. That is why, before the Big Bang gained currency, so many leading scientists were keen to dismiss it, since it seemed to support the Bible story. Some clung to Aristotle's view of the "eternal universe" without beginning or end; but this theory, and later variants of it, are now discredited.

Hawking, however, contents himself with saying:

> According to the Old Testament, God created Adam and Eve only six days into creation. Bishop Ussher, primate of all Ireland from 1625 to 1656, placed the origin of the world even more precisely, at nine in the morning on October 27, 4004 BC. We take a different view: that humans are a recent creation but that the universe itself began much earlier, about 13.7 billion years ago.[37]

It is clear that Hawking, though he has thought in depth about the interpretation of the data of science, has not thought very seriously about the interpretation of the biblical data. Some might think that resting content with Ussher's interpretation of the Bible is like resting content with Ptolemy's interpretation of the universe with its fixed earth and all the heavenly bodies rotating around it – something which Hawking would not dream of doing.

---

[37] Op. cit. p. 124.

If Hawking had engaged a little more with biblical scholarship, rather than simply putting the biblical creation account into the same pigeonhole as Norse, Mayan, Africana and Chinese myths, he might have discovered that the Bible itself leaves the time of creation open. In the structure of the text of Genesis, the statement "in the beginning God created the heavens and the earth" does not form part of the creation "week" but clearly precedes it; and so, however one interprets the days of creation, neither the age of the earth nor that of the universe is specified; and so there is no necessary conflict between what Genesis says and the 13.7 billion years yielded by scientific calculation.

As Hawking points out, the first actual scientific evidence that the universe had a beginning did not appear until the early 1900s. The Bible, however, has been quietly asserting that fact for millennia. It would be good if credit were given where it is due.

3 *God or the multiverse?*

In trying to avoid the evidence that is visible to all for the existence of a divine intelligence behind nature, atheist scientists are forced to ascribe creative powers to less and less credible candidates, like mass/energy, the laws of nature, or even to their theories about those laws. In fact, Hawking has not only not got rid of God, he has not even got rid of the God of the Gaps in which no sensible person believes. For the very theories he advances to banish the God of the Gaps are themselves highly speculative and untestable.

Like every other physicist, Hawking is confronted with powerful evidence of design:

> Our universe and its laws appear to have a design that both is tailor-made to support us and, if we are to exist, leaves little room for alteration. That is not easily explained and raises the natural question of why it is that way ... The discovery relatively recently of the extreme fine-tuning of so many of the laws of nature could lead at least some of us back to the old idea that this grand design is the work of some grand designer ... That is not the answer of modern science ... our universe seems to be one of many, each with different laws.[38]

---

[38] Op. cit. pp. 162, 164.

It is therefore quite clear that Hawking recognizes a "Grand Design". He devotes almost an entire chapter to giving extensive details of the spectacular fine-tuning of both the laws of nature and the constants associated with fundamental physics. The evidence he gives is impressive, and certainly fits in with what he calls the "old idea that this grand design is the work of some grand designer". Of course it does: it fits like a glove – because there is a Grand Designer.

The idea of a Grand Designer is certainly *old*, but the important question to ask is whether or not it is *true*. Simply to say it is old can give the erroneous impression that what is old is necessarily false and has been superseded. Secondly, it can give the further incorrect impression that no one holds it today. However, as we have seen, some of the finest minds in science do hold it. The conviction that there is a Grand Designer, God, the Creator, is held by millions, if not billions of people – vastly more, incidentally, than those who hold the atheist alternative.

The multiverse

Hawking, therefore, goes too far in claiming that the existence of a Grand Designer is not the answer of modern science. What, then, is Hawking's preferred answer to what he admits is the "apparent miracle" (of fine-tuning)?

It is the multiverse. The idea is, roughly speaking, that there are several many-world scenarios, and so many universes (some suggest infinitely many, whatever that means) that anything that can happen will happen in some universe. It is not surprising then, so the argument goes, that there is at least one universe like ours.

We note in passing that Hawking has once again fallen into the trap of offering false alternatives. This time it is: God or the multiverse. From a theoretical point of view, as philosophers have pointed out, God could create as many universes as he pleases. The multiverse concept *of itself* does not and cannot rule God out.[39] Hawking does not seem to have provided us with any argument to counter this observation.

In addition, leaving aside other universes, the physical constants in this universe are fine-tuned. They could have been otherwise, so the theory of the multiverse does not, in any case, annul the evidence of God's "Grand Design" that is to be perceived in this universe.[40]

What of the multiverse itself? Is it fine-tuned? If it is, then Hawking is back where he started.[41] Where is Hawking's argument to prove that it is not?

With his multiverse Hawking moves out beyond science into the very realm of philosophy, whose death he announced rather prematurely. As Paul Davies points out: "All cosmological models are constructed by augmenting the results of observations by some sort of philosophical principle."[42]

Furthermore, there are weighty voices within science that are not as enthusiastic about the multiverse. Prominent among them is that of Sir Roger Penrose,

---

[39] See, for instance, Robin Collins' contribution in Bernard Carr (ed.), *Universe or Multiverse?*, Cambridge, Cambridge University Press, 2007, chapter 26.

[40] For an accessible account of the relationship of this statement to the "Inverse Gambler's Fallacy" see Phil Dowe, *Galileo, Darwin and Hawking*, Grand Rapids, Wm B. Eerdmans, 2005, pp. 160ff.

[41] See Bernard Carr, op. cit. p. 464.

[42] Bernard Carr, op. cit. p. 487.

Hawking's former collaborator, who shared with him the prestigious Wolf Prize. Of Hawking's use of the multiverse in *The Grand Design* Penrose said: "It's overused, and this is a place where it is overused. It's an excuse for not having a good theory."[43] Penrose does not, in fact, like the term "multiverse", because he thinks it is inaccurate: "For although this viewpoint is currently expressed as a belief in the parallel co-existence of different alternative worlds, this is misleading. The alternative worlds do not really 'exist' separately, in this view; only the *vast particular superposition* ... is taken as real."[44]

John Polkinghorne, another eminent theoretical physicist, rejects the multiverse concept:

Let us recognize these speculations for what they are. They are not physics, but in the strictest sense, metaphysics. There is no purely scientific reason to believe in an ensemble of universes. By construction these other worlds are unknowable by us. A possible explanation of equal intellectual respectability – and to my mind greater economy and elegance – would be that this one world is the way it is, because it is the creation of the will of a Creator who purposes that it should be so.[45]

I am tempted to add that belief in God seems to be a much more rational option, if the alternative is to believe that every other universe that can possibly exist does exist; including one in which Richard Dawkins is the

43 Premier Christian Radio, "Unbelievable" with Justin Brierley, 25 September 2010.
44 Op. cit. p. 784.
45 *One World*, London, SPCK, 1986, p. 80.

Archbishop of Canterbury, Christopher Hitchens the Pope, and Billy Graham has just been voted atheist of the year!

M-theory

To be serious once more (but perhaps I was being serious), Hawking's ultimate theory to explain why the laws of physics are as they are is called M-theory: a theory of supersymmetric gravity that involves very sophisticated concepts, such as vibrating strings in eleven dimensions. Hawking confidently calls it the "unified theory that Einstein was expecting to find". If it is, it will be a triumph of mathematical physics; but, for the reasons given above, far from administering the death-blow to God, it will give us even more insight into his creatorial wisdom. Don Page, a theoretical physicist from the University of Alberta, who is a former student of Hawking and has co-authored eight papers with him, says: "I certainly would agree that even if M-theory were a fully formulated theory (which it isn't yet) and were correct (which of course we don't know), that would not imply that God did not create the universe."[46]

Once again it needs to be stressed that M-theory is an abstract theory, and not a creator. It describes a scenario (or, more accurately, a series of scenarios, as it is a family of theories) that has solutions which allow for 10^{500} different universes[47] – assuming of course that M-theory is true, which is by no means certain, as we shall see. However, even if it is true, *M-theory itself doesn't*

---

46 Private communication, reproduced with permission.
47 Op. cit. p. 118.

create a single one of those universes. What Hawking says is: "The laws of M-theory allow for different universes with different apparent laws." "Allow for" is one thing, "create" is something completely different. A theory that allows for many universes is not the same as an agent who designed them, or a mechanism that produces them.

What is very interesting in all of this is the impression being given to readers of *The Grand Design* that God is somehow rendered unnecessary, or non-existent, by science. Yet when one examines the arguments one can see that the intellectual cost of doing so is impossibly high, since it involves an attempt to get rid of the Creator by conferring creatorial powers on something that is not in itself capable of doing any creating – an abstract theory.

Tim Radford captures this very cleverly in his review of *The Grand Design*:

> In this very brief history of modern cosmological physics, the laws of quantum and relativistic physics represent things to be wondered at but widely accepted: just like biblical miracles. M-theory invokes something different: a prime mover, a begetter, a creative force that is everywhere and nowhere. This force cannot be identified by instruments or examined by comprehensible mathematical prediction, and yet it contains all possibilities. It incorporates omnipresence, omniscience and omnipotence, and it's a big mystery. Remind you of Anybody?[48]

---

[48] Tim Radford, *The Guardian*, 18 September 2010.

A similar point had already been made by physicist Paul Davies: "The general multiverse explanation is simply naïve deism dressed up in scientific language. Both appear to be an infinite unknown, invisible and unknowable system. Both require an infinite amount of information to be discarded just to explain the (finite) universe we observe."[49]

The validity of M-theory

Although it does not affect my argument, it should be noted that not all physicists are as convinced as Hawking about the validity of M-theory, and they have been quick off the mark to say so. For instance, theoretical physicist Jim Al-Khalili says:

> The connection between this multiverse idea and M-theory is, however, tentative. Advocates of M-theory such as Witten and Hawking would have us believe that it is done and dusted. But its critics have been sharpening their knives for a few years now, arguing that M-theory is not even a proper scientific theory if it is untestable experimentally. At the moment it is just a compelling and beautiful mathematical construct, and in fact only one of a number of candidate TOEs [Theories of Everything].

Paul Davies says of M-theory: "It is not testable, not even in any foreseeable future."[50] Oxford physicist Frank Close goes further: "M-theory is not even defined

49   Bernard Carr, op. cit. p. 495.
50   Hannah Devlin, *The Times*, 4 September 2010.

... we are even told 'No one seems to know what the M stands for.' Perhaps it is 'myth'." Close concludes: "I don't see that M-theory adds one iota to the God debate, either pro or con."[51] Jon Butterworth, who works at the Large Hadron Collider in Switzerland, states: "M-theory is highly speculative and certainly not in the zone of science that we have got any evidence for."[52]

Before the appearance of Hawking's book Roger Penrose wrote some cautionary words:

It has been a not uncommon view among confident theoreticians that we may be "almost there", and that a "theory of everything" may lie not far beyond the subsequent developments of the late twentieth century. Often such comments had tended to be made with an eye on whatever had been the status of the "string theory" that had been current at the time. It is harder to maintain such a viewpoint now that string theory has transmogrified to something (M- or F-theory) whose nature is admitted to being fundamentally unknown at present.

Penrose continues:

From my own perspective, we are much farther from a "final theory" even than this ... Various remarkable *mathematical* developments have indeed come out of string-theoretic (and related) ideas. However, I remain profoundly unconvinced that they are very much other than just striking

51 'Science. Life. The Planet', *The Times, Eureka*, Issue 12, September 2010, p. 23

52 Hannah Devlin, *The Times*, 4 September 2010.

pieces of mathematics albeit with input from some deep physical ideas. For theories whose space-time dimensionality exceeds what we directly observe (namely 1+3), I see no reason to believe that, in themselves, they carry us much further in the direction of *physical* understanding.[53]

In a radio discussion with Alister McGrath after the appearance of Hawking's book, Penrose was even more forthright.[54] Asked whether science shows that the universe could "create itself from nothing" Penrose responded with a strong condemnation of the string theory that Hawking espouses: "It's certainly not doing it yet. I think the book suffers rather more strongly than many. It's not an uncommon thing in popular descriptions of science to latch onto an idea, particularly things to do with string theory, which have absolutely no support from observation. They are just nice ideas." He stated that M-theory was "very far from any testability ... It's a collection of ideas, hopes, aspirations." Referring directly to *The Grand Design*, he then said: "The book is a bit misleading. It gives you this impression of a theory that is going to explain everything; it's nothing of the sort. It's not even a theory." Indeed, in Penrose's estimation, M-theory was "hardly science".[55]

It should be noted that Penrose's criticisms are scientific and do not arise from any religious convictions. He is, in fact, a member of the British Humanist Association.

53 *The Road to Reality*, London, Jonathan Cape, 2004, p. 1010.
54 Premier Christian Radio, "Unbelievable" with Justin Brierley, 25 September 2010.
55 Roger Penrose has developed his own theory in his new book *Cycles of Time*, Oxford, Bodley Head, 2010.

In Hawking's view, a model is a good model if it:

- is elegant;
- contains few arbitrary or adjustable elements;
- agrees with and explains all existing observations;
- makes detailed predictions about future observations that can disprove or falsify the model if they are not borne out.[56]

Comparing these criteria with the comments about M-theory above, it is unclear why M-theory is the good model that Hawking appears to think it is. Accounting for the fine-tuning of the cosmos by postulating one intelligent Creator seems much more elegant and economical than postulating 10^{500} different universes that are unobservable by us, and is surely a much better "model".

A move to advance the cause of atheism by means of a highly speculative, untestable theory that is not within the zone of evidence-based science, and which, even if it were true, could not dislodge God in any case, is not exactly calculated to impress those of us whose faith in God is not speculative, but testable and well within the zone of evidence-based rational thought.

Modelling reality: the nature of perception

Since Hawking understands M-theory to be a model, it is important to say a few words about Chapter 3 of his book, where he explains his view of mathematical theories as models. Using an analogy of a goldfish that

---

[56] Op. cit. p. 51.

sees the world through the distorting lens of its bowl, Hawking affirms:

> There is no picture- or theory-independent concept of reality. Instead we will adopt a view that we will call model-dependent realism: the idea that a physical theory or world picture is a model (generally of a mathematical nature) and a set of rules that connect the elements of the model to observations ... According to model-dependent realism, it is pointless to ask whether a model is real, only whether it agrees with observations.[57]

Roger Penrose is less convinced by this anti-realism. Referring to Hawking's stance, he writes: "My own position, on the other hand, is that the issue of ontology is crucial to quantum mechanics, though it raises some matters that are far from being resolved at the present time."[58] In his review of *The Grand Design* he records his antipathy to subjectivity:

> Among Einstein's difficulties with current quantum mechanics was its leading to *subjective* pictures of physical reality – as abhorrent to him as to me. The viewpoint of "theory-dependent realism" being espoused in this book appears to be a kind of half-way house, objective reality being not fully abandoned, but taking different forms depending upon the particular theoretical perspective it is viewed from, enabling the possibility of equivalence between black and white holes.

[57] Op. cit. pp. 42, 46.
[58] *The Road to Reality*, p. 785.

Penrose then comments on the "goldfish bowl":

> An illustrative example the authors provide involves goldfish trying to formulate a theory of the physical space outside their spherical goldfish bowl. The external room appears to them to have curved walls, despite being regarded as rectilinear by its human inhabitants. Yet the goldfish's and human's viewpoints are equally consistent, providing identical predictions for those physical actions accessible to both life forms at once. Neither viewpoint is more real than the other, being equivalent for making predictions.
>
> I do not see what is new or "theory-dependent" about this perspective on reality. Einstein's general theory of relativity already deals with such situations in a completely satisfactory way, in which different observers may choose to use different co-ordinate systems for local descriptions of the geometry of the single fixed over-reaching objective space-time. There is a degree of subtlety and sophistication in the mathematics, going significantly beyond what is present in Euclid's ancient geometry of space. *But the mathematical "space-time", whereby the theory describes the world, has complete objectivity* [italics mine].
>
> It is nevertheless true that current quantum theory presents threats to this objectivity of classical physics (including general relativity) and has not yet provided an accepted universally objective picture of reality. In my opinion, this reflects an incompleteness in current quantum theory, as was also Einstein's view. It is likely that any

"completion" of quantum theory to an objective picture of reality would require new mathematical ideas of subtlety and sophistication beyond even that of Einstein's general-relativistic space-time, but this challenge is addressed to future theorists' ingenuity and does not, in my view, *represent any real threat to the existence of an objective universe* [italics mine]. The same might apply to M-theory, but unlike quantum mechanics, M-theory enjoys no observational support whatever.[59]

Hawking's view of reality is derived from what he thinks about human perception. He says that perception is "not direct, but rather is shaped by a kind of lens, the interpretive structure of our human brains".[60] Hawking is now entering one of the most complex and difficult areas of philosophy, the realm of epistemology. Epistemology has to do with theories of knowledge – how we know what we know, and with what justification. Epistemology challenges us to consider how far our prejudices, values, and even our methods of scientific investigation limit or even distort the impressions we receive.

For instance, we see from quantum mechanics that the very means used to investigate elementary particles so affects those particles that the scientist cannot simultaneously determine both the location and the velocity of any one particle. It is also well known that a scientist's personal world-view can affect the interpretation he places on the results of his experiments, and on the theories he forms.

---

59 Review in *Financial Times*, 4 September 2010.
60 Op. cit. p. 46.

The aspect of epistemology at issue here is perception. Philosophers seek to understand the actual process that is going on when we perceive something in the external world; and even at this primary level there is already a difference of opinion. At one extreme in the debate stands *Naïve*, or *Direct, Realism*. It asserts that, under normal conditions, we have direct perception of the external world. I see a tree, for instance, and I perceive its existence and its qualities simply by looking directly at it, touching it, smelling it even.

At the other extreme in the debate stands the *Representative Theory of Perception* (RTP). It asserts that we never perceive a tree, or anything else, directly. When we look at a tree, what happens is that our minds receive certain subjective impressions or representations of the tree; and it is these subjective representations – called *sense-data* – that we directly and most immediately perceive, not the objective tree itself. And it is on these sense-data that we depend for our knowledge of the tree. Some philosophers who espouse this theory liken it to watching a football match, not directly, but on a television screen. But this theory does not claim that we are necessarily conscious of these subjective sense-data, as we would be of a television screen; or that we formally infer from the sense data the existence and the features of the tree. But nonetheless it maintains that this is what is really happening: what we perceive are simply these subjective sense-data, not the tree itself, and our knowledge of the tree is built on them.

The implication of this theory should now be clear. If it were true, we could never check the accuracy of our subjective impressions of the objective world against the objective world itself, because, however much we studied the objective world, we would never perceive it itself, but only some subjective impression of it. We might decide that one set of sense-data was better than another (though by what standard should we judge?); but we could never be sure that any set of sense-data represented the objective reality with complete accuracy.

It would seem that Hawking adopts something very like the Representative Theory of Perception. Now it is simply not possible to branch off into a detailed discussion of epistemology in this book. I shall content myself by coming back to Hawking's goldfish in a bowl analogy, because it is our visual perception that is often appealed to in order to justify RTP. For instance, a straw in a glass of water looks bent at the surface of the water.

However, concentrating solely on visual perception could be misleading. In addition to our five senses we have reason and memory, and often two or more senses can be applied together. Memory and reason can join them simultaneously to achieve direct and correct perception. Let's do a simple mental experiment to show that this is so.

Suppose we stand in the middle of a straight railway track. As we look along the track the two rails will appear to converge in the distance, until we can no longer distinguish them. At that moment our sense-data will record that they have coalesced. Presently a train comes up behind us. We step out of the way and the train goes by. As it recedes into the distance the train appears to get smaller and, according to RTP, our sense-data will duly record an ever-diminishing train.

But now reason and memory come into play. Reason tells us that locomotives cannot get smaller just by travelling (unless they approach the speed of light!); and memory of trains on which we have travelled reminds us that trains don't get smaller as they proceed. So now, although our visual perception sees the train getting smaller, we know that it is actually the same size as when it passed us. That means that, as we watch the train reach the distant point where the rails looked as if they coalesce (and still do in our sense-data), we can use the known size of the locomotive as a means of measuring the distance between the two rails at that point, and know with total confidence that, in spite of appearance, the rails are the same distance apart there as where we are standing.

Moreover, all this is going on in our heads simultaneously. Initial visual perception suggested that the rails were coalescing. Now visual perception allows us to see what happens when the train reaches the point of apparent coalescence: we can see that the train does not come to a halt but keeps going. Simultaneously, reason perceives with absolute certainty that the rails cannot have coalesced but are as far apart as usual. In other words, it is not necessarily true that vision always produces subjective sense-data which reason subsequently turns into valid concepts, as one version of RTP suggests. In a knowledgeable person, reason and memory can work alongside vision to help achieve the true perception of objective reality.

Commenting on RTP, philosopher Roger Scruton writes:

> It seems to say that we perceive physical objects only by perceiving something else, namely, the idea or image that represents them. But then,

how do we perceive that idea or image? Surely
we shall need another idea, which represents it
to consciousness, if we are to *perceive* it? But now
we are embarked on an infinite regress. Wait
a minute, comes the reply; I didn't say that we
perceive mental representations as we perceive
physical objects. On the contrary, we perceive the
representations *directly*, the objects only *indirectly*.
But what does that mean? Presumably this: while
I can make mistakes about the physical object, I
cannot make mistakes about the representation,
which is, for me, immediately incorrigible,
self-intimating – part of what is "given" to the
consciousness. But in that case, why say that I
perceive it at all? Perception is a way of finding
things out; it implies a separation between the
thing perceiving and the thing perceived, and
with that separation comes the possibility of
error. To deny the possibility of error is to deny
the separation. The mental representation is
not perceived at all; it is simply *part* of me. Put
it another way: the mental representation *is* the
perception. In which case, the contrast between
direct and indirect perception collapses. We do
perceive physical objects, and perceive them
directly ... And we perceive physical objects by
having representational experiences.[61]

In other words, there is no third, intermediate and
quasi-independent thing called sense-data between
our perception and objects in the external world. The

---

61 Roger Scruton, *Modern Philosophy*, London, Arrow Books, 1996 edition, p. 333.

sense-data, or representations, are our perception of the external world; and that perception of the world is direct. That does not mean, of course, that direct perception is never mistaken. The fact is that, when it comes to using our senses to gain information about the external, objective world, human beings have had to learn to use their five senses correctly, and interpret the information correctly. Each one of us has to do so individually. Someone may hear a musical sound, as sound-waves enter his ear and then his brain, and yet misjudge the musical instrument from which it has come. Experience, sight, instruction, and memory will all be necessary before he can immediately recognize the instrument. But that doesn't mean that originally he didn't hear the sound directly. A person recently blinded will need to develop an increasingly sensitive touch in order to read Braille. And, since light behaves in the way we now know it does, we have to learn to see and how to gather correct information from eyesight. From time to time we can misinterpret what we see, hear, touch, taste and smell, and we have to learn to use our senses with greater discernment. But none of this means that we cannot have direct perception of anything at all in the external world, whatever additional difficulties we may have at the quantum level.

Finally, if we cannot directly perceive that Hawking and Mlodinow are objectively real people who have written a book called *The Grand Design*, which makes certain truth claims about the universe, then one would wonder why they bothered to write it in the first place. And that is just the interesting thing about those who espouse various kinds of relativism: they all seem to end up by saying, essentially, that truth, perception, etc. are relative, except of course the truth they are passionately trying to get us to perceive. That is, they fail to apply their own relativism to themselves.

The subjective element in science

It is, of course, important to recognize that there is a subjective element in science. The idea of a completely independent observer, free of all preconceived theories, doing investigations and coming to unbiased conclusions that constitute absolute truth, is simply a myth. For, in common with everyone else, scientists have preconceived ideas, indeed world-views, that they bring to bear on every situation. Furthermore, they are well aware that it is almost impossible for them to make any kind of observation without resting on some prior theory; for example, they cannot even take a temperature without having an underlying theory of heat. Also, their scientific theories tend to be underdetermined by the data; that is, more than one theory could account for the same set of data. If, for example, we plot our observational data on a graph as a finite set of points, elementary mathematics will tell us that there is no limit to the number of curves that we can draw through that particular set of points. That is, the data represented by the points on the paper do not determine the curve that we should draw through them, although in any particular case, there may well be physical principles that significantly restrict our choice.

Most scientists will freely admit, therefore, that science, by its very nature, possesses an inevitable degree of tentativeness. It needs to be made clear, however, that the degree of this tentativeness is extremely small in the vast majority of cases. The fact is that science-based technology has been spectacularly successful in fundamentally changing the face of the world: from radio and television to computers, aircraft, space probes, X-rays and artificial hearts. It is sheer nonsense, therefore, to assert, as postmodernists often do, that these elements of tentativeness and subjectivity in science mean that science is a purely social construct. As physicist Paul Davies says:

> Of course, science has a cultural aspect; but if I say that the planets moving around the sun obey an inverse-square law of gravitation and I give a precise mathematical meaning to that, I think it is really the case. I don't think it is a cultural construct – it's not something we have invented or imagined just for convenience of description – I think it's a fact. And the same for the other basic laws of physics.[62]

It is self-evident, surely, that if we believed that the science that led to the construction of jet aircraft was merely a subjective social construct, none of us would ever get on a plane. Or, to put it another way, one sure method of finding out whether the law of gravity is a social or cultural construct or not would be to step off the top of a skyscraper!

---

[62] "Found in space?" Interview with Paul Davies, *Third Way*, July 1999.

4 Whose design is it anyway?

In the final chapter of their book, Hawking and Mlodinow discuss the "Grand Design". They open the chapter by saying that although the laws of nature tell us *how* the universe behaves, they do not answer the *why* questions they posed at the start of the book: Why is there something rather than nothing? Why do we exist? Why this particular set of laws and not another?[63] So far, so good. The laws of nature do not answer the why questions. However, as we saw in Chapter 2, the conclusion of the book contradicts this by affirming that the laws of nature, and in particular the law of gravity, do provide the answer to these questions.

To make sure we have got this right, let us remind ourselves of that conclusion: "Because there is a law like gravity the universe can and will create itself from nothing ... Spontaneous creation is the reason there is something rather than nothing, why the universe exists, why we exist."[64] There it is in black and white. The law of gravity is the answer to the very questions that Hawking says it cannot answer.

Furthermore, what does Hawking mean by "spontaneous creation"? It sounds very much like an uncaused cause, an expression often cited as a paradoxical

63 Op. cit. p. 171.
64 Op. cit. p. 180.

way of describing God. And, even if there were such a thing as spontaneous creation it would scarcely be a *reason*, would it? A reason would be something that replaced the dots in the statement "There is something rather than nothing *because*...". Hawking's statement seems to be saying: "There is something rather than nothing *because* there is something – and that something comes about spontaneously without any cause or reason except, maybe, that it is possible and just happens."

It is hard to be impressed by this kind of argument – especially when it is compounded by the multiple self-contradictions mentioned earlier.

If, on the other hand, we turn to God as the answer to the why questions, as I unashamedly do, then Hawking will counter: "It is reasonable to ask who or what created the universe, but if the answer is God, then the question has merely been deflected to that of who created God."[65]

Well, what is sauce for the goose is sauce for the gander. If the answer is "the law of gravity" (which, as we have already seen in Chapter 2, it cannot be), by Hawking's own argument the question has merely been deflected to: who created the law of gravity? And this is a question that he does not answer.

Hawking is here giving an argument that serves only to reveal the inadequacy of his concept of God. To ask the question who *created* God logically presupposes that God is a created entity. That is certainly not the Christian – nor, indeed, the Jewish or Muslim – concept of God. God is eternal; he is the ultimate reality, the ultimate fact. To ask who created him is to show that one does not understand the nature of his being.[66]

---

65 Op. cit. p. 172.

66 I consider this matter in greater depth in *God's Undertaker*, pp. 182ff.

Austin Farrer comments aptly on what is at stake here: "The issue between the atheist and the believer is not whether it makes sense to question ultimate fact, it is rather the question: what fact is ultimate? The atheist's ultimate fact is the universe; the theist's ultimate fact is God."[67] Maybe we should modify this to say that for some atheists the ultimate fact is the multiverse, or the law of gravity, but this makes no difference to the point at issue.

The bulk of Hawking's final chapter is devoted to an example of a mathematical model that, according to him, creates a reality of its own: John Conway's "Game of Life". Conway envisioned a "world" consisting of an array of squares like a chess board, but extending indefinitely in all directions. Each square can be in one of two states, "alive" or "dead", represented by the squares being coloured green or black respectively. Each square has eight neighbours (up, down, left, right and four on the diagonals). Time moves in discrete steps. You start with any chosen arrangement of alive and dead squares; there are three rules or laws that determine what happens next, all proceeding deterministically from the initial chosen state. Some simple patterns remain the same, others change for several generations and then die out; yet others return to their original form after several generations and then repeat the process indefinitely. There are "gliders", consisting of five alive squares, which morph through five intermediate shapes and then return to their original shape, albeit displacing one square along the diagonal. And there are many more sophisticated forms of behaviour exhibited by more complex initial configurations.

67 Austin Farrer, *A Science of God*, London, Geoffrey Bles, 1966, pp. 33-34.

Part of Conway's world (remember that it is assumed infinite in all directions) can be modelled on a computer, so that one can watch what happens as generation succeeds generation. For instance, "gliders" can be observed crawling diagonally across the screen.[68]

This world with its simple laws holds great attraction for mathematicians, and has been instrumental in the development of the important theory of cellular automata. Conway and his students, as Hawking points out, showed that there are complex initial configurations that self-replicate under the laws. Some of them are so-called Universal Turing Machines that can, in principle, carry out any calculation that could be carried out on a computer. Configurations of alive and dead squares in Conway's world that are able to do this have been calculated as being of enormous size – consisting of trillions of squares.[69]

As a mathematician, I find Conway's work fascinating. Listening to him make mathematics come alive was one of the high points of my experience of Cambridge lectures. However, what interests me here is Hawking's purpose in using this analogy:

> The example of Conway's Game of Life shows that even a very simple set of laws can produce complex features similar to those of life. There must be many sets of laws with this property. What picks out the fundamental laws (as opposed to the apparent laws) that govern our universe? As in Conway's universe, the laws of our universe

[68] To see what this looks like visit http://en.wikipedia.org/wiki/Conway%27s_Game_of_Life.
[69] See http://rendell-attic.org/gol/utm/index.htm.

determine the evolution of the system given the state at any one time. In Conway's world we are the creators – we choose the initial state of the universe by specifying objects and their positions at the start of the game.

Hawking continues: "In a physical universe, the counterparts of objects such as gliders in the Game of Life are isolated bodies of matter."[70]

At this point Hawking diverts from the Game of Life, and leaves the reader uncertain as to exactly how he is applying it. Nevertheless, one can surely say that the impression has been communicated to the reader that, just as in Conway's world a simple set of laws can produce lifelike complexity, in our world a simple set of laws could produce life itself.

However, the analogy shows nothing of the sort, but rather the exact opposite. First of all, in Conway's world the laws do not produce the complex self-replicating objects. Laws, as we have constantly emphasized, create nothing in any world: they can only act on something that is already there. In Conway's world the immensely complex objects that can self-replicate under the laws have to be initially configured in the system by highly intelligent mathematical minds. They are created neither from nothing nor by chance, but by intelligence. The same applies to the laws.

Secondly, Conway's world has to be implemented, and this is done using sophisticated computer hardware with all its attendant software and high-speed algorithms. The alive and dead cells are represented by pixellated squares on a screen, and the laws governing their behaviour are programmed into the system. It should go without saying – but it clearly needs to be said – that all of this involves massive intellectual activity and input of information.

In this way, even though he is allergic to the notion of intelligent design,[71] Hawking has just given an excellent argument in its support. Ironically, he actually admits this by saying that, in Conway's world, we are the creators.

And in our universe the Creator is God.

71 Op. cit. p. 164.

5 Science and rationality

Much of the rationale behind Hawking's argument lies in the idea that there is a deep-seated conflict between science and religion. This is not a discord that I recognize. For me, as a Christian believer, the beauty of the scientific laws reinforces my faith in an intelligent, divine Creator. The more I understand science the more I believe in God, because of my wonder at the breadth, sophistication, and integrity of his creation.

Indeed, the very reason that science flourished so vigorously in the sixteenth and seventeenth centuries, under men like Galileo, Kepler and Newton, had a great deal to do with their conviction that the laws of nature reflected the influence of a divine law-giver. One of the fundamental themes of Christianity is that the universe was built according to a rational, intelligent design. Far from belief in God hindering science, it is the motor that drove it.

The fact that science is (mainly) a rational activity helps us to identify another flaw in Hawking's thinking. Like Francis Crick, he wants us to believe that we human beings are nothing but "mere collections of fundamental particles of nature". Crick writes: "You, your joys and your sorrows, your memories and ambitions, your sense of personal identity and free will, are in fact no more than the behaviour of a vast assembly of nerve cells and their associated molecules."[72]

---

72 *The Astonishing Hypothesis: The Scientific Search for the Soul*, London, Simon and Schuster, 1994, p. 3.

What shall we think, then, of human love and fear, joy and sorrow? Are they meaningless neural behaviour patterns? Or, what shall we make of the concepts of beauty and truth? Is a Rembrandt painting nothing but molecules of paint scattered on canvas? Hawking and Crick would seem to think so. One wonders, then, by what means we should recognize it. After all, if the concept of truth itself results from "no more than the behaviour of a vast assembly of nerve cells", how in the name of logic would we know that our brain was composed of nerve cells?

These arguments recall what has come to be known as Darwin's Doubt: "With me, the horrid doubt always arises whether the convictions of man's mind, which has been developed from the mind of the lower animals, are of any value or at all trustworthy."

By far and away the most devastating criticism of such extreme reductionism is that, like scientism, it is self-destructive. Physicist John Polkinghorne describes its programme as:

> ultimately suicidal. If Crick's thesis is true we could never know it. For, not only does it relegate our experiences of beauty, moral obligation, and religious encounter to the epiphenomenal scrapheap, it also destroys rationality. Thought is replaced by electro-chemical neural events. Two such events cannot confront each other in rational discourse. They are neither right nor wrong. They simply happen... The very assertions of the reductionist himself are nothing but blips in the neural network of his brain. The world of rational discourse dissolves into the absurd chatter of firing

synapses. Quite frankly, that cannot be right and none of us believes it to be so.[73]

Precisely. There is a patent self-contradiction running through all attempts, however sophisticated they may appear, to derive rationality from irrationality. When stripped down to their bare bones, they all seem uncannily like the futile attempts to lift oneself by one's bootstraps that we mentioned in the first chapter. After all, it is the use of the human mind that has led Hawking and Crick to adopt a view of human beings that carries with it the corollary that there is no reason to trust our minds when they tell us anything at all; let alone, in particular, that such reductionism is true.

The very existence of the capacity for rational thought is surely a pointer: not downwards to chance and necessity, but upwards to an intelligent source of that capacity. We live in an information age, and we are well aware that language-type information is intimately connected with intelligence. For instance, we have only to see a few letters of the alphabet spelling our name in the sand to recognize at once the work of an intelligent agent. How much more likely, then, is the existence of an intelligent Creator behind human DNA, the colossal biological database that contains no fewer than 3.5 billion "letters" – the longest "word" yet discovered?

However, we are now moving away from physics in the direction of biology – a subject in which similar issues arise. I have devoted a great deal of attention to it in my book *God's Undertaker*, so I shall not re-tell that story here.

---

[73] *One World*, pp. 92–93.

Rational support for the existence of God from outside science

Rational support for the existence of God is not only to be found in the realm of science, for science is not co-extensive with rationality, as many people imagine. For instance, we find ourselves to be moral beings, capable of understanding the difference between right and wrong. There is no scientific route to such ethics, as has been admitted by all but the most die-hard converts to scientism. Physics cannot inspire our concern for others, nor was science responsible for the spirit of altruism that has existed in human societies since the dawn of time. But that does not mean that ethics is non-rational.

Furthermore, just as the fine-tuning of the constants of nature and the rational intelligibility of nature point to a transcendent intelligence that is independent of this world, so the existence of a common pool of moral values points to the existence of a transcendent moral being.

History is also a very important rational discipline. Indeed, it is easy to overlook the fact that the methods of the historian have a very important role to play within science itself. We have been discussing the way in which the universe is describable in terms of physical law, and most of us are aware that physical laws are often established by an inductive process. That is, observations can be repeatedly made, experiments repeatedly done,and, if they give the same results each time under the same conditions, we feel comfortable in asserting that we have a genuine law, by what we call "inductive inference". For instance, we can repeatedly observe the motion of the planets in their orbits round the sun, and thus confirm Kepler's laws of planetary motion.

In areas of science such as cosmology, however, there are things which we cannot repeat. The most obvious example is the history of the universe from its beginning. We cannot re-run the Big Bang and say that it has been established by repeated experimentation.

What we can and do employ are the methods of the historian. We use a procedure called "inference to the best explanation" (or "abductive inference").[74] We are all familiar with this procedure, since it is the key to every good detective novel. A is murdered. B is found to have a motive – she stood to profit if A died. So B did it? Maybe. But then C is found to have had a violent row with A on the night he was murdered. So C did it? Maybe. But then... and Hercule Poirot keeps us guessing until the final denouement. Let us call the circumstance where there are several possible hypotheses consistent with an observed outcome the Poirot Principle.

The point about a Poirot story is that you cannot re-run the murder to see who did it. We cannot, therefore, expect the same level of certainty here which we get with repeated experimentation. It is that very feature, of course, that makes Poirot stories so enjoyable.

Exactly the same thing happens in cosmology. We set up a hypothesis. Suppose there was a Big Bang, and let's call this hypothesis A. We then say: if A happened, what would we expect to find today? Someone says: we would expect to find B. So, scientists look and find B. What does this prove? Well, it is consistent with A, but it does not prove that A happened with the same kind of certainty that is associated with inductive argument, for the very obvious reason that there could be another hypothesis,

---

74 For further discussion see Alister McGrath, *A Scientific Theology: Reality*, Edinburgh, T & T Clark, 2002, pp. 157ff.

A^1 – very different from A, but nevertheless consistent with observing B. Indeed, there could be many other hypotheses different from A but consistent with observing B. The Poirot Principle operates in cosmology.

It is for this reason that inference to the best explanation (abduction) does not carry the same weight as inductive inference. M-theory is speculative. Kepler's laws are not. The danger is that, because science involves both induction and abduction, the latter is often invested with the authority accorded to the former.

Nevertheless, inference to the best explanation plays a very important role in those branches of science that deal with unrepeatable events in the past; like the origin of the universe and of life.

It is perfectly appropriate, therefore, to turn to history to ask if it supplies us with any evidence that there is a God. After all, if there is a God who is ultimately responsible for this universe and human life, it would surely not be surprising if he were to reveal himself. One of the main reasons I believe in God is because of the evidence that God has revealed himself to human beings within recorded history. The evidence centres mainly on the life and work of Jesus Christ, and focuses above all on his resurrection from the dead, which is presented to us as a fact of history.

These events are well attested in the biblical record, whose authenticity has been repeatedly established. There are also important extra-biblical sources and a wealth of archaeological findings that confirm the reliability of the biblical narrative. My faith in God, therefore, rests not only on the testimony of science but also on the testimony of history, particularly to the fact that Jesus Christ rose from the dead.

Here we are once again in the realm of the singular and unrepeatable; and, in light of Hume's dictum cited above, we shall clearly require strong evidence, if belief in the resurrection is to be credible. However, Hawking will stop us at this point, and object that my claim that the resurrection occurred violates one of the fundamental principles of science: the laws of nature are universal – they admit no exceptions. As we have seen, Hawking is quite prepared to make inferences to the best explanation about unrepeatable past events. In his view, however, the resurrection is impossible in principle.

Hawking discusses this in the context of his convictions about what he calls "scientific determinism" – a view traceable to Laplace. "Given the state of the universe at one time, a complete set of laws fully determines both the future and the past. That would exclude the possibility of miracles or an active role for God."[75]

On the basis of his determinism, Hawking reduces biology to physics and chemistry and concludes: "It is hard to see how free will can operate if our behaviour is determined by physical law, so it seems we are no more than biological machines and that free will is just an illusion."[76] He concedes, however, that human behaviour is so complex that predicting it would be impossible, so in practice we use "the effective theory that people have free will".[77]

Hawking says: "This book is rooted in the concept of scientific determinism which implies that… there are no miracles, or exceptions to the laws of nature."[78] Could it

[75] Op. cit. p. 30.
[76] Op. cit. p. 32.
[77] Op. cit. p. 33.
[78] Op. cit. p. 34.

be his scientific determinism that is the illusion? He is explicit in defining the implications of his determinism. In connection with the difficulty of predicting human behaviour in practice, he says, in a statement again reminiscent of Laplace: "For that one would need a knowledge of each of the initial states of each of the thousand trillion trillion molecules in the human body and to solve something like that number of equations."[79] At first sight this seems like strange language to come from a contemporary expert on quantum theory, which has as one of its fundamental tenets the Heisenberg Principle of Indeterminacy – that it is not possible simultaneously to measure accurately the position and the momentum of an electron, say. This principle would appear to vitiate any possibility of realizing Laplace's deterministic dream, even in theory.

However, Hawking has not forgotten the Uncertainty Principle. In a later chapter he informs us that the Uncertainty Principle "tells us that there are limits to our ability to simultaneously measure certain data, such as the position and velocity of a particle".[80] This leads him at once to modify his original "scientific determinism".

Quantum physics might seem to undermine the idea that nature is governed by laws, but that is not the case. Instead, it leads us to accept a new sort of determinism: given the state of a system at some time, the laws of nature determine the *probabilities* of various futures and pasts rather than determining the future and past with certainty.[81]

[79] Op. cit. p. 32.
[80] Op. cit. p. 70.
[81] Op. cit. p. 72.

His absolute determinism seems to have been seriously diluted – by Hawking himself. How, or even whether, he thinks this modified "determinism" (if that's what it is) negates free will and the possibility of miracles, he does not say.

Let us, therefore, cite a comment on the implications of determinism by another physicist, John Polkinghorne.

> In the opinion of many thinkers, human freedom is closely connected with human rationality. If we were deterministic beings, what would validate the claim that our utterance constituted rational discourse? Would not the sounds issuing from mouths, or the marks we made on paper, be simply the actions of automata? All proponents of deterministic theories, whether social and economic (Marx), or sexual (Freud), or genetic (Dawkins and E. O. Wilson), need a covert disclaimer on their own behalf, excepting their own contribution from reductive dismissal.[82]

It would appear, therefore, that Hawking's name would be a suitable addition to this list.

Miracles and the laws of nature

According to Hawking, then, the reign of the laws of nature is absolute. They determine everything and permit no exceptions. There can therefore be no miracles. He writes: "These laws should hold everywhere and at

[82] *Science and Theology*, London, SPCK, 1998, p. 58.

all times; otherwise they wouldn't be laws. There could be no exceptions or miracles. Gods or demons couldn't intervene in the running of the universe." [83]

Once again we are faced with a choice between mutually exclusive alternatives. Either we believe in miracles or we believe in the scientific understanding of the laws of nature, but not both.

Not surprisingly, this argument is also put forward with characteristic force by Richard Dawkins:

> The nineteenth century is the last time when it was possible for an educated person to admit to believing in miracles like the virgin birth without embarrassment. When pressed, many educated Christians are too loyal to deny the virgin birth and the resurrection. But it embarrasses them because their rational minds know that it is absurd, so they would much rather not be asked. [84]

However, it cannot be quite as simple as Hawking and Dawkins think. There are highly intelligent, eminent scientists who would differ with them; for instance: Professor William Phillips, Physics Nobel Prizewinner 1998; Professor John Polkinghorne FRS, Quantum Physicist, Cambridge; Sir John Houghton, former Director of the British Meteorological Office and Head of the International Governmental Panel on Climate Change; and the current Director of the National Institute of Health and former Director of the Human Genome Project, Francis Collins. These distinguished scientists are well aware of the arguments against miracles.

---

[83] Op. cit. p. 171.
[84] *The God Delusion*, p. 187.

Nevertheless, publicly and without embarrassment or a sense of absurdity, each affirms his belief in the supernatural and, in particular, in the resurrection of Christ – which they regard, as I do, as the supreme evidence for the truth of the Christian world-view.

One of the scientists just mentioned, Francis Collins, gives a wise caution regarding the matter of miracles:

> It is crucial that a healthy scepticism be applied when interpreting potentially miraculous events, lest the integrity and rationality of the religious perspective be brought into question. The only thing that will kill the possibility of miracles more quickly than a committed materialism is the claiming of miracle status for everyday events for which natural explanations are readily at hand.[85]

For that reason I shall concentrate on the resurrection of Christ, in order to give the discussion as sharp a focus as possible. It was the miracle of the resurrection of Christ that started Christianity going, and that same miracle is its central message. Indeed, the basic qualification of a Christian apostle was to be an eyewitness of the resurrection.[86] C. S. Lewis writes: "The first fact in the history of Christendom is a number of people who say they have seen the Resurrection. If they had died without making anyone else believe this 'gospel', no Gospels would ever have been written."[87] According to the early Christians, then, without the resurrection there simply is no Christian message. The apostle Paul writes: "If Christ

85 *The Language of God*, pp. 51–52.
86 Acts 1:22.
87 *Miracles*, London, Fount Paperbacks, 1974, p. 148.

has not been raised, our preaching is useless and so is your faith."[88]

Let us remind ourselves of the perspective of contemporary science, and its thinking about the laws of nature. Since scientific laws embody cause-effect relationships, scientists nowadays do not regard them as merely capable of describing what has happened in the past. Provided we are not working at the quantum level, such laws can successfully predict what will happen in the future with such accuracy that, for example, the orbits of communication satellites can be precisely calculated, and moon and Mars landings are possible. Many scientists are therefore convinced that the universe is a closed system of cause and effect.

In light of this, it is understandable that such scientists resent the idea that some god could arbitrarily intervene and alter, suspend, reverse, or otherwise "violate", these laws of nature. To them that would seem to contradict the immutability of those laws, and thus overturn the very basis of the scientific understanding of the universe. In consequence many such scientists would advance the following two arguments against miracles.

The first is that belief in miracles in general, and in the New Testament miracles in particular, arose in primitive, pre-scientific cultures, where people were ignorant of the laws of nature and so readily accepted miracle stories.

Any initial plausibility which this explanation may seem to possess disappears rapidly when it is applied to New Testament miracles like the resurrection. A moment's thought will show us that, in order to recognize

---

[88] 1 Corinthians 15:14.

some event as a miracle, there must be some perceived regularity to which that event is an apparent exception! You cannot recognize something as abnormal if you do not know what is normal.

This was actually well appreciated long ago, indeed at the time of the writing of the New Testament documents. Interestingly, the historian Luke, who was a doctor trained in the medical science of his day, raises this very matter. In his account of the rise of Christianity, Luke informs us that the first opposition to the Christian message of the resurrection of Jesus Christ came not from atheists, but from the high priests of Judaism. They were highly religious men of the party of the Sadducees. They believed in God. They said their prayers and conducted the services in the Temple. But that did not mean that the first time they heard the claim that Jesus had risen from the dead they believed it. They did not believe it, for they had embraced a world-view which denied the possibility of bodily resurrection of anyone at all, let alone that of Jesus Christ.

Indeed, they shared a widespread conviction. Historian Tom Wright says:

Ancient paganism contains all kinds of theories, but whenever resurrection is mentioned, the answer is a firm negative: we know that doesn't happen. (This is worth stressing in today's context. One sometimes hears it said or implied that prior to the rise of modern science people believed in all kinds of odd things like resurrection but that now, with two hundred years of scientific research on our side, we know that dead people stay dead. This is ridiculous. The evidence, and the conclusion, was massive and massively drawn in the ancient world as it is today.)[89]

To suppose, then, that Christianity was born in a pre-scientific, credulous, and ignorant world is simply false to the facts. The ancient world knew the law of nature as well as we do, that dead bodies do not get up out of graves. Christianity won its way by dint of the sheer weight of evidence that one man had actually risen from the dead.

The second objection to miracles is that now we know the laws of nature, miracles are impossible. This is Hawking's position. However, it involves a further fallacy that C. S. Lewis illustrated with the following analogy:

If this week I put a thousand pounds in the drawer of my desk, add two thousand next week and another thousand the week thereafter, the laws of arithmetic allow me to predict that the next time I come to my drawer, I shall find four thousand pounds. But suppose when I next open the drawer, I find only one thousand pounds, what shall I conclude? That the laws of arithmetic have been broken? Certainly not! I might more reasonably conclude that some thief has broken the laws of the State and stolen three thousand pounds out of my drawer. One thing it would be ludicrous to claim is that the laws of arithmetic make it impossible to believe in the existence of such a thief or the possibility of his intervention. On the contrary, it is the normal workings of those laws that have exposed the existence and activity of the thief.[90]

---

[89] James Gregory Lecture, University of Durham, 2007.
[90] *Miracles*, p. 62.

The analogy also reminds us that the scientific use of the word "law" is not the same as the legal use, where we often think of a law as constraining someone's actions. There is no sense in which the laws of arithmetic constrain or pressurize the thief in our story. Newton's law of gravitation tells me that if I drop an apple it will fall towards the centre of the earth. But that law does not prevent someone intervening, and catching the apple as it descends. In other words, the law predicts what will happen, provided there is no change in the conditions under which the experiment is conducted.

Thus, from the theistic perspective, the laws of nature predict what is bound to happen if God does not intervene. It is no act of theft, of course, if the Creator intervenes in his own creation. To argue that the laws of nature make it impossible for us to believe in the existence of God and the likelihood of his intervention in the universe is plainly false. It would be like claiming that an understanding of the laws of the jet engine would make it impossible to believe that the designer of such an engine could, or would, intervene and remove the fan. Of course he could intervene. Moreover, his intervention would not destroy those laws. The very same laws that explained why the engine worked with the fan in place would now explain why it does not work with the fan removed.

It is, therefore, inaccurate and misleading to say with David Hume that miracles "violate" the laws of nature. Once more C. S. Lewis is helpful:

If God annihilates or creates or deflects a unit of matter, He has created a new situation at that point. Immediately all nature domiciles this new situation, makes it at home in her realm, adapts all other events to it. It finds itself conforming to all the laws. If God creates a miraculous spermatozoon in the body of a virgin, it does not proceed to break any laws. The laws at once take over. Nature is ready. Pregnancy follows, according to all the normal laws, and nine months later a child is born.[91]

In this vein we could say that it is a law of nature that human beings do not rise again from the dead *by some natural mechanism*. But Christians do not claim that Christ rose from the dead by such a mechanism. This point is of vital importance for the whole discussion: they claim that he rose from the dead by supernatural power. By themselves, the laws of nature cannot rule out that possibility. When a miracle takes place, it is the laws of nature that alert us to the fact that it is a miracle. It is important to grasp that Christians do not deny the laws of nature. It is an essential part of the Christian position to believe in the laws of nature as descriptions of those regularities and cause-effect relationships which have been built into the universe by its Creator, and according to which it normally operates. If we did not know them, we should never recognize a miracle if we saw one. The crucial difference between the Christian view and Hawking's view is that Christians do not believe that this universe is a closed system of cause and effect. They believe that it is open to the causal activity of its Creator God.

In anybody's book then, miracles, by definition, are exceptions to what normally happens. They

91 *Miracles*, p. 63.

are singularities. However, it is one thing to say: "Experience shows that such and such normally happens, but there may be exceptions, although none has been observed; that is, the experience *we have had up to this point has been uniform*." It is an entirely different thing to say: "This is what we normally experience, and we must always experience it, for there can be and are no exceptions."

However, Hawking appears committed to the view that nature is absolutely uniform: the laws of nature know no exceptions. We have seen that the laws of nature cannot forbid miracles. So how does Hawking know that they cannot happen? In order to know that experience against miracles is *absolutely* uniform, he would need to have total access to every event in the universe at all times and places, which is self-evidently impossible. Humans have only ever observed a tiny fraction of the sum total of events that have occurred in the universe; and very few of the total of all human observations have been written down. Therefore, Hawking cannot know that miracles have never occurred in the past, or that they might occur in the future. He is simply assuming what he wants to prove. He is expressing a belief based on his atheistic worldview, not on his science.

The problem here is that the uniformity of nature, sometimes called the inductive principle, on which much scientific argument is based, cannot be proved. We noted earlier that David Hume had pointed this out. Alister McGrath argues that "it is an unjustified (indeed, circular) assumption within any non-theistic world-view".[92] McGrath cites no less an authority than the famous atheist philosopher Bertrand Russell:

> Experience might conceivably confirm the inductive principle as regards the cases that have been already examined; but as regards unexamined cases, it is the inductive principle alone that can justify an inference from what has been examined to what has not been examined. All arguments, which, on the basis of experience, argue as to the future or the unexperienced parts of the past or present, assume the inductive principle; hence we can never use experience to prove the inductive principle without begging the question. Then we must either accept the inductive principle on the ground of its intrinsic evidence, or forgo all justification of our expectation about the future.[93]

The only rational alternative to such a circular argument, of course, is to be open to the possibility that miracles have occurred. That is a historical question, and not a philosophical one, and depends on witness and evidence. But there is nothing in Hawking's book that suggests that he is willing to consider the question of whether there is any valid historical evidence that a miracle like the resurrection has taken place. Perhaps history, like philosophy, is also dead?

I agree, of course, that miracles are inherently improbable – although one cannot help wondering if they are as improbable as universes popping into existence from nothing. We should certainly demand strong

---

92 *A Scientific Theology: Reality*, p. 153.

93 *The Problems of Philosophy*, Oxford, Oxford University Press, 1998, p. 78.

evidence for the occurrence of any particular miracle. But this is not the real problem with miracles of the sort found in the New Testament. The real problem is that they threaten the foundations of the world-view of naturalism, which holds as an axiom that nature is all that there is, and that there is nothing and no one outside nature that could from time to time intervene in nature. That axiom is not a consequence of scientific investigation. It might just be a consequence of fear that God might somehow penetrate the atheists' inadequate radar.

Ironically enough, Christians will argue that it is *only belief in a Creator that gives us a satisfactory ground for believing in the uniformity of nature (the inductive principle) in the first place*. In denying that there is a Creator, the atheists are kicking away the basis of their own argument! As C. S. Lewis puts it:

> If all that exists is Nature, the great mindless interlocking event, if our own deepest convictions are merely the by-products of an irrational process, then clearly there is not the slightest ground for supposing that our sense of fitness and our consequent faith in uniformity tell us anything about a reality external to ourselves. Our convictions are simply a fact about us – like the colour of our hair. If Naturalism is true we have no reason to trust our conviction that Nature is uniform. It can be trusted only if quite a different metaphysic is true. If the deepest thing in reality, the Fact which is the source of all other facthood, is a thing in some degree like ourselves – if it is a Rational Spirit and we derive our rational spirituality from It – then indeed our conviction

can be trusted. Our repugnance to disorder is derived from Nature's Creator and ours.[94]

Thus, excluding the possibility of miracle, and making Nature and its processes an absolute in the name of science, ends up by removing all grounds for trusting in the rationality of science, let alone the uniformity of nature, in the first place. On the other hand, regarding nature as only part of a greater reality, which includes nature's intelligent Creator God, gives a rational justification for belief in the orderliness of nature. It was this conviction that led to the rise of modern science. McGrath once more: "The idea that nature is governed by 'laws' does not appear to be a significant feature of Greek, Roman or Asian conceptions of science; it is firmly entrenched within the Judaeo-Christian tradition, reflecting the specifics of a Christian doctrine of creation."[95]

However, in order to account for the uniformity of nature, if one admits the existence of a Creator, the door is inevitably open for that same Creator to intervene in the course of nature. There is no such thing as a tame Creator who cannot, or must not, or dare not actively get involved in the universe he has created. Miracles may occur.

Incidentally, is it not rather odd that Hawking believes in the multiverse and rejects miracles? Isn't the whole point about multiverses to have enough universes around to ensure that *anything* can happen? Physicist

[94] *Miracles*, p. 109.

[95] Op. cit. p. 154. The reader interested in pursuing (the considerable) philosophical and scientific debate on the status of the laws of nature is encouraged to look at the relevant sections of McGrath's work.

Paul Davies explains:

> Consider the most general multiverse theories ...
> where even laws are abandoned and anything at
> all can happen. At least some of these universes
> will feature miraculous events – water turning
> into wine, etc. They will also contain thoroughly
> convincing religious experiences, such as direct
> revelation of a transcendent God. It follows that a
> general multiverse set must contain a subset that
> conforms to traditional religious notions of God
> and design.[96]

Similarly, according to philosopher Alvin Plantinga
of Notre Dame University, if every possible universe
exists, then there must be a universe in which God
exists, since his existence is logically possible. It then
follows that since God is omnipotent and omnipresent
he must exist in every universe; hence there is only
one universe, this universe, of which he is the Creator
and upholder!

If Stephen Hawking is going to avoid God, perhaps
the multiverse is not the wisest hiding place after all.

The upshot of all this is that science does not, indeed,
cannot rule out miracle. Surely, then, the open-minded
attitude demanded by reason is to proceed now to
investigate the evidence, to establish the facts, and be
prepared to follow where that process leads; even if it
entails alterations to our preconceived ideas. We shall
never know whether or not there is a mouse in the attic
unless we actually go and look! The problem is, some

---

[96] Bernard Carr (ed.), op. cit. p. 495.

people are more afraid of finding God than they are of finding mice.

Just one more word about Hume. It is worth remembering that, in spite of his objections to miracles, he wrote: "The whole frame of nature bespeaks an intelligent author; and no rational enquirer can, after serious reflection, suspend his belief a moment with regard to the primary principles of genuine Theism and Religion."[97]

A final comment

Science and history are not the only sources of evidence for the existence of God. Since God is a Person and not a theory, it is to be expected that one of the prime evidences for his existence is personal experience. To develop this important matter, it would take us far beyond the intended scope of this little book. Nevertheless I wish to add my voice to the many millions who can and would testify to the profound and central role that faith in Christ as Lord has on our lives, bringing assurance of peace with God, a new power for living, and a certain hope based on the resurrection of Christ. Such a hope defies both the death barrier and Hawking's bleak reductionist notion that we are nothing more than a random collection of molecules derived from the stars. We shall, in fact, outlast the stars.

Hawking imagines that the potential existence of other life forms in the universe undermines the traditional religious conviction that we are living in a unique, God-created planet. I find it faintly amusing that atheists often

---

[97] From the introduction to *The Natural History of Religion* (with an Introduction by John M. Robertson), London, A. and H. Bradlaugh Bonner, 1889.

argue for the existence of extra-terrestrial intelligence beyond earth.[98] They are only too eager to denounce the possibility that there exists a vast, intelligent being "out there", namely God, who has left his fingerprints all over his creation.

Hawking's fusillade will not shake the foundations of an intelligent faith that is based on the cumulative evidence of science, history, the biblical narrative, and personal experience.

[98] For an extensive discussion, see Paul Davies, *The Eerie Silence: Are We Alone in the Universe?*, London, Allen Lane, 2010.

Conclusion

I am under no illusion that I have covered all the topics I might or should have covered in this short book. Not only that, many of the topics that have been mentioned deserve much more consideration. I do hope, however, that I have at least managed to communicate to you that the widespread belief that atheism is the default intellectual position is untenable. More than that, I hope that for many of you this investigation of Hawking's atheistic belief system will serve to confirm your faith in God, as it has mine, and that it will encourage you not to be ashamed of bringing God into the public square by joining in the debate yourself.

I even dare to hope that, for some of you, this little book may be the start of a journey that will eventually lead to your coming to believe in the God who not only made the universe but also conferred on you the immeasurable dignity of creating you in his image, with the capacity for thought and the intellectual curiosity that got you reading this book in the first place. In turn that could even be, as it was for me, the first step in embarking on what is by definition life's highest adventure – getting to know the Creator through the Son that has revealed him.

John C. Lennox

Oxford, October 2010